CONFLICT MANAGEMENT IN HEALTHCARE

"Filled with practical examples and exercises to practice skills, *Conflict Management in Healthcare* is an easy-to-follow guide addressing one of the most critical needs in healthcare—conflict resolution. The CCGA process is intuitive yet refreshing in its design to preserve personal integrity and grow trust between team members even in times of conflict. The powerful pairing of the CCGA with the CLARC system of communication effectively addresses interpersonal conflict (in both personal and professional settings), and can be used to help leaders effectively mediate conflict in their teams. Best of all, these systems can be customized to the unique healthcare systems!"

—Melissa Childress, Vice President of Cancer Services, Winship Cancer Institute and Emory Healthcare, Atlanta, GA

"Years ago, I had the opportunity to work in a hospital and realized the culture and environment were different than what I expected. What I needed was this book, *Conflict Management in Healthcare: Creating a Culture of Cooperation*. Healthcare professionals are compassionate and caring. They deal with change regularly, and those attempts tend to lead to some level of conflict. The authors have created a beneficial resource for healthcare change agents as they navigate COVID and the 'new norm.'"

—Dr. Marie Gould Harper, Dean of Dr. Wallace E. Boston School of Business, American Public University System

"Today, in the midst of the COVID pandemic, when people's nerves are at their limit, when doctors and medical staff are working under increased pressure, the need to be able to respond to the challenges of conflict is particularly relevant. In *Conflict Management in Healthcare: Creating a Culture of Cooperation*, healthcare practitioners have been given tools to resolve different types of conflicts in hospitals, operating rooms, and inpatient departments. This publication is valuable not only to doctors, nurses, administrators, and other healthcare staff, but should become a priceless manual for medical students and residents."

—Dr. Leon Aguliansky, MD, Surgeon-Urologist, Assuta Rishon Medical Center

"If you are a healthcare leader looking to more effectively manage conflict in your organization, *Conflict Management in Healthcare: Creating A Culture of Cooperation* is a 'must read.' The authors have incorporated tips and tools to inspire better team communication in an industry fueled by emotions and challenged by pace. This should be required reading for any healthcare leader that understands effective employee communication should be a high organizational priority."

—Kelly Hurt, DH, Vice President CHRO, Southeast Health Administration

"*Conflict Management in Healthcare: Creating a Culture of Cooperation* is a roadmap to help healthcare professionals navigate the world of escalating demands, work overload, and recurring conflict among medical stakeholders. It is particularly important for senior managers and coordinators who manage different types of healthcare activities."

—Prof. Maria Sierpinska, Chancellor, University of Economics and Human Sciences in Warsaw, Economic Counsellor of Prime Minister of Poland

"*Conflict Management in Healthcare: Creating a Culture of Cooperation* should be required reading for all leaders, both formal and informal, in today's challenging healthcare settings. Crisp, concise, and practical, the authors provide a framework to address and resolve conflict in these complex organizations with instruments, approaches, and techniques that can proactively support, beyond best intentions, organizational alignment and effectiveness in service to the mission, vision, and values of the organization."

—Jon C. Abeles, EdD, Former Senior Vice President, Catholic Health Partners

"The world's healthcare organizations are confronted with a raging global pandemic. Healthcare professionals are fighting the COVID-19 virus heroically to save lives, cultures, and countries. Central to this epic health crisis is the conflict. While conflict can be destabilizing in any context, Dr. McDaniel's book provides usable strategies, tactics, and tools enabling healthcare professionals to harness the power and potential inherent in conflict. This book establishes the global standard for conflict management in healthcare hallmarked by collaboration, cooperation, and compassion."

—Michael Williams, PhD, Dean, College of Business, Thomas Edison State University

"The authors of *Conflict Management in Healthcare* present a practical and rational approach to conflict which emerges from a stressful and challenging environment. I strongly recommend this book not only to managers and healthcare workers but also to students and junior doctors who begin their rewarding yet extremely demanding work at health facilities."

—Prof. Malgorzata Sobieszczanska, Dean of the Faculty of Medicine, Head of Department and Clinic of Geriatrics at Wroclaw Medical University, Poland

"Whether we are care recipients, caregivers, subject-matter experts, family members living far away, clinicians on the front lines, staff support in long-term care centers, top executives in healthcare company headquarters, or from any other walk of life, healthcare affects us all. Without a doubt we all need and deserve smooth sailing on our healthcare navigation. We need to be able to maneuver within cooperative cultures, and I strongly encourage reading and using *Conflict Management in Healthcare: Creating a Culture of Cooperation* as an ongoing roadmap. It is smart and sensible, thorough, practical, and worthy of repeat reads as personal healthcare situations change. Most especially the Conflict-Management Style Survey is a terrific and easy-to-take tool for getting where we need and want to be during our own healthcare journeys and experiences."

—Melody Chatelle, PhD, Owner, Chatelle and Associates, Author of *Journeys of Heartache and Grace: Conversations and Life Lessons from Young People with Serious Illnesses*

"Healthcare professionals hold in their hands the most precious things—human beings' health and life; thus, they are expected to do their best every day. However, this sort of work is extremely exhausting and stressful, so interpersonal conflicts on various levels are unavoidable. Not many professionals are good at solving this sort of problem, and such skills are still not enough developed during medical education. This excellent book can be a wise, helpful guide in managing conflicts for both healthcare employees and administration. The knowledge provided by this book will lead you to better cooperation and make your work more satisfactory and effective for you and your patients!"

—Professor Grzegorz Mazur, MD, PhD, Head of Department and Clinic of Internal Medicine, Occupational Diseases, Hypertension and Clinical Oncology, Wroclaw University Hospital

"Healthcare, like so many worthwhile enterprises, requires a team to deliver great care.

With so many different disciplines and professions (not to mention diverse backgrounds), it's only natural that conflict arises. In my experience, healthcare providers often avoid conflict—which festers and worsens—and/or they need better skills to effectively resolve the conflict. These situations have significant implications for the quality and safety of patient care and the long-term engagement of staff. This book provides a comprehensive roadmap for resolving conflicts in healthcare, and the concepts are readily transferable to other fields."

—Marcia Silverberg, President, HR Directions

"Healthcare organizations are entities whose environment, by its very nature, is characterized by a high probability of conflict situations. Conflict results from the importance of decisions made in particularly exceptional circumstances for all stakeholders, including staff, patients, and their families. The potential for conflict increases even more as societies become more aware of service quality requirements and diagnostics and treatment possibilities provided by technological progress. *Conflict Management in Healthcare: Creating a Culture of Cooperation* provides practical solutions to overcome this problem. It provides clear guidance for the direction healthcare-sector entities should go in terms of conflict management in stakeholders' growing expectations. This publication will be useful for both managers and healthcare professionals, especially where the organizational culture is not yet well established. It will support the shift to a proactive approach, seeking to eliminate unproductive disputes by creating a culture that engages conflict."

—Lukasz Czajkowski, Development Projects and Marketing Department Manager, Latawiec Hospital

"Compliments to Garry McDaniel and his team for providing this insightful, targeted, and well-written analysis of how conflict in the healthcare environment generates mistrust and negatively impacts patients, staff, and leadership to compromise the quality of care. This timely book should be at the top of the reading list of every healthcare executive and care team member to stimulate self-reflection and guide change."

> —Jeannette E. South-Paul, MD, DHL (Hon), FAAFP, Professor and Chair Emeritus, Family Medicine, University of Pittsburgh School of Medicine

"Management and employees frequently fail to work with each other and deal with conflict effectively because they lack the skills and a system for doing so. If management and employees do not share standards of conduct and behavior, have no process for addressing problems and conflicts, and lack effective communications skills, why should we not expect a high level of discord? *Conflict Management in Healthcare* will provide your institution and employees with the framework they need to enhance patient care, build trust, and reduce conflict."

> —Mateusz Samoraj, PhD, Director of Agrochemicals Technology and Product Development in EKOPLON, Assistant Professor at Wroclaw University of Science and Technology, Poland

"Read this book to get a peek into the future of conflict resolution in the healthcare field and how to apply this cutting-edge paradigm to ensure you're developing a positive work culture. The shift is as dramatic and fundamental as analog to digital. Dr. McDaniel and his co-authors provide a roadmap to sustainability and profitability for the next iteration of business models. Brilliant work!"

> —Susan Rieser, CEO, Thrive Massage and Wellness

"*Conflict Management in Healthcare: Creating a Culture of Cooperation* addresses the cognitive dissonance which permeates healthcare and other workplaces. It offers pragmatic strategies and tools to go beyond cooperation to achieve trusting, productive, and mutually beneficial relationships and outcomes in difficult and tense settings. Its utility extends far beyond the healthcare setting and applies wherever organizational culture clashes with organizational realities."

—Barry Silverberg, Director, Austin: Center for Nonprofit Studies at Austin Community College and Co-principal, Silverberg Associates

"*Conflict Management in Healthcare: Creating A Culture of Cooperation* is a valuable and timely contribution in a field of growing concern, and provides an in-depth, well-organized examination of varieties of conflict influencing quality of service faced daily by medical management clinicians. This book introduces new areas of discussion and should be of interest to all members of the healthcare community."

—Liza Canowitz, CNM, BSN

Conflict Management in Healthcare:

Creating a Culture of Cooperation

By Garry McDaniel, EdD
with
Gary Stroud, PhD
Leslie Mathew, MD
Mikhail Dernakovski, MD
Alex Batsenko, MD
Siddarth Agrawal, MD

© Copyright 2021 Garry McDaniel, EdD

ISBN 978-1-64663-214-5

All rights reserved. No part of this publication may be reproduced, stored in a retrieval system, or transmitted in any form or by any means—electronic, mechanical, photocopy, recording, or any other—except for brief quotations in printed reviews, without the prior written permission of the author.

Published by

köehlerbooks™

3705 Shore Drive
Virginia Beach, VA 23455
800-435-4811
www.koehlerbooks.com

CONFLICT MANAGEMENT
IN HEALTHCARE

Creating a Culture of Cooperation

Garry McDaniel, EdD
WITH Gary Stroud, PhD, Leslie Mathew, MD,
Mikhail Dernakovski, MD, Alex Batsenko, MD,
AND Siddarth Agrawal, MD

VIRGINIA BEACH
CAPE CHARLES

TABLE OF CONTENTS

ACKNOWLEDGMENTS 1
FOREWORD 3
HOW TO USE THIS BOOK 9

Chapter 1

THE CONFLICT-MEDIATION SYSTEM 12

LEADERSHIP and CONFLICT 13
PRODUCTIVE vs. UNPRODUCTIVE CONFLICT 18
THE COST of UNPRODUCTIVE CONFLICT 19
RESPONDING to CONFLICT 27
    Method One: Avoidance 28
    Method Two: Accommodation 29
    Method Three: Compromise 29
    Method Four: Competing 30
    Method Five: Cooperation 31
CAUSES of UNPRODUCTIVE CONFLICT 33
THE VALUE of COOPERATION 39
THE CONFLICT-MEDIATION SYSTEM 41

CHAPTER 1 TOOLS AND ACTIVITIES 45
Conflict-Management Style Survey 45
Assessing Your Organization's Level of Conflict 49

Chapter 2

STANDARDS OF BEHAVIOR AND CONDUCT.......... 51

SHARED ORGANIZATIONAL VALUES 57
POWER MANAGEMENT 61
PROCESS LEADERSHIP 63
CREATING A SAFE ENVIRONMENT 64
APPRECIATING DIVERSITY 67
THE SYNERGY of STANDARDS 69
VIOLATING STANDARDS 76
    Bullying 78
    Harassment 80
CHAPTER 2 TOOLS and ACTIVITIES.............. 85
    Assessing Standards of Conduct and Behavior...... 85

Chapter 3

THE CONFLICT-CONCERNS-GOALS-ACTIONS

PROCESS 86

CONFLICT-MEDIATION PROCESS 89
    Step One: Identify the Conflict 92
    Step 2: Clarify Concerns......................... 93
    Step 3: Identify Your Goals 96
    Step 4: Action Plan.............................. 97
FOLLOW the CCGA CYCLE 98
DIAGRAMMING the CCGA PROCESS 99
CASE STUDY #1: ROMANTIC NIGHT OUT 100
CASE STUDY #2: WORK TEAM 103
CHAPTER 3 TOOLS AND ACTIVITIES.............. 110

Chapter 4

COMMUNICATION SKILLS 112

CONFRONT 113
LISTEN 116
ACKNOWLEDGE 119
RESPOND 122
COMMIT 124
APPLYING the CLARC SKILLS 125
CHAPTER 4 TOOLS and ACTIVITIES 127
    Personal Communications Skills Inventory 127
    Organizational Communications Skills Audit 128
    Activities for Building Trust and Understanding..... 130
        Preparing for Potential Hot Spots 130
        Zen Counting..................................... 130
        "Who's got a dollar?" Exercise 131

Chapter 5

COACHING OTHERS EXPERIENCING CONFLICT 133

CONFLICT and COACHING 135
FOLLOW-UP COACHING 139
GROUP COACHING 141
    Group-Conflict Coaching Example 142
CHAPTER 5 TOOLS and ACTIVITIES 147
    Personal-Coaching Map 147

Chapter 6
IMPLEMENTING THE CONFLICT-MEDIATION SYSTEM..148

WHY CUSTOMIZE?....................................151
CUSTOMIZATION PROCESS..........................151
    Step One: Create a Steering Team 153
    Step Two: Create an Inspirational Culture 154
    Step Three: Identify Training Needs...............159
    Step Four: Develop Implementation Plan 161
    Step Five: Pilot and Improve Training 162
    Step Six: Implement 162
    Step Seven: Plan for the Future...................163
    Step Eight: Monitor and Communicate Results......163
CASE EXAMPLE #3: ANGELS of MERCY 165
WHAT IF PEOPLE STILL CAN'T SOLVE
CONFLICT THEMSELVES? 169
CONCLUDING THOUGHTS............................172
CHAPTER 6 TOOLS and ACTIVITIES...................175
    Implementation Process Worksheet................175

Chapter 7
MANAGING EVERYDAY CONFLICT...................176

FAMILY and CONFLICT MEDIATION 177
CONFLICTS with FRIENDS............................182
CONFLICT MEDIATION and COMMUNITY GROUPS 185
CHAPTER 7 TOOLS and ACTIVITIES...................191
    Life-Events Worksheet...........................191
    Personal-Conflict Diagram.......................193

Chapter 8

TAKING THE NEXT STEP 194

EFFECTIVE COMMUNICATION 195
COOPERATION 196
FLEXIBILITY. 197
EMPLOYEE EXPERIENCE 198
CONFLICT and GROWTH 198
CHAPTER 8 TOOLS and ACTIVITIES 201
    Conversations about Culture 201
    Assess Your Willingness to Act 203

CONFLICT CASES 205
BIBLIOGRAPHY 211
ABOUT THE AUTHORS 212

ACKNOWLEDGMENTS

Very few worthy *endeavors* come to fruition without the support and encouragement of others. Our book is certainly no exception. The authors of this book would like to thank our colleagues, friends, and family members who provided guidance, stories, and reassurance during the process of writing this book. We particularly want to thank the dedicated professionals in the healthcare industry. Caring for others every day, year after year, in stressful, often life-or-death situations is draining, but clearly a gratifying calling. We are honored to work with these amazing professionals to ensure the culture of healthcare organizations is one of respect, care, collective purpose, and civility.

FOREWORD

> *You never change things by fighting the existing reality. To change something build a new model that makes the existing model obsolete.*
> —Richard Buckminster Fuller

Healthcare organizations are struggling with increasing expectations, escalating demands for services, and a high degree of scrutiny from patients, politicians, insurance companies, and the public. As a result, there is a clear need to maximize the performance and cohesion of the people in the organizations at every level. The resources and infrastructure available to the healthcare system in the United States are some of the best in the world. This enormous system consists of dentists, doctors, nurses, protective care and nursing facilities, pharmacies, allied medical health services, hospitals, home healthcare services, outpatient departments, diagnostic laboratories, and veterinary clinics as well as pharmaceutical companies. Collectively, these organizations provide access to care, therapies, and treatments that help contribute to a longer and higher quality of life for the population of the United States.

A central principle of the healthcare profession is caring for others; do no harm. Where many organizations in the healthcare profession struggle is not in available resources and infrastructure; it is with delivery of services. To be clear, delivery of good services is rarely a problem of knowledge or skills. The healthcare professionals providing service have all the talent and ability they need to provide the best level of care. The challenge is in ensuring that the organizational culture values care internally for all employees as much as it does for the customer or patient. The principle of care must be a bedrock foundation of the systems, process, and behaviors of everyone.

Our reasoning for this sentiment is simply that if employees experience unproductive conflict through incivility, harassment, hazing, bullying, or demeaning behaviors, they do not work together and communicate as effectively. This directly influences quality of service. Healthcare professionals must keep unproductive conflict at a minimum if they are to provide the level of care patients need as well as quality products and services while working in very difficult work environments characterized by the demand for extraordinary quality, exacting standards of practice, increasing levels of public and governmental oversight, and managing costs of care. Managing conflict in such a demanding and dynamic workplace is a time-consuming but necessary task for all employees and an obligation of administration.

Conflict occurs between physicians, physicians and staff, administrators and management, management and direct reports, and between healthcare providers and the patient or patient's family. While many people tend to think of *conflict* as something to be avoided, the fact is that conflict often leads to positive outcomes. We learn what we are doing wrong, or about some process, procedure, or behavior that we can implement better, and this all leads to improvement, learning, positive change, growth, new ideas, better relationships, and increased trust. This is *productive conflict*.

Unproductive conflict, on the other hand, is characterized by frequent, repetitive arguments, and disagreements that are not resolved and leave those involved feeling angrier and more frustrated than they were before. Unproductive conflict may also stem from behaviors or actions that are disrespectful, bullying, or harassing in nature. In healthcare organizations, unproductive conflict may range from minor disagreements to major controversies leading to mistakes, wasted resources, litigation, or even violence. The result is that unproductive conflict has an adverse effect on productivity, morale, the reputation of the institution, and patient care. Work environments characterized by too much unproductive conflict or an inability to deal constructively with conflict suffer from high employee turnover, lower morale, poor communication, and absenteeism that can impede efficient delivery of care or delivery of quality products or services.

The authors of this book will be the first to acknowledge that while all employees (top to bottom) can and should learn the skills needed to communicate and resolve conflict effectively, training is not a "magic bullet" that will solve this problem. In fact, we suspect that if you are working in today's demanding healthcare environment, you have probably already attended workshops or seminars on the topic of conflict management. In addition, your organization may have offered additional training programs in communication skills, team development, interpersonal relationships, coaching, facilitation, and management skills. Given all of these learning opportunities, you would think the lives of employees in the healthcare profession would be free of unproductive conflict! Creating a workplace in which employees deal effectively with productive and unproductive conflict requires developing and sustaining a culture where all employees feel safe, respected, and have the skills they need to interact well with others.

The title of this book, *Conflict Management in Healthcare: Creating a Culture of Cooperation*, reflects our belief and experience that everyday conflict can be turned into opportunities for enhancing interpersonal, team, and organizational relationships. It also reflects the Joint Commission's belief that there is a difference between conflict management and conflict engagement. The Joint Commission observes that *conflict management* is an overall approach to conflict that includes skill building, non-adversarial process design, and conflict resolution. Creating a culture that *engages* conflict from a positive perspective takes this proactive stance one step further (Scott and Gerardi 2011). Conflict engagement refers to the ability to effectively enter into and address conflicts of various types, at various depths, and over differing periods, ranging from short-lived interactions to more complex and protracted disputes. From this perspective, conflict is viewed as inevitable and natural; conflict is an opportunity, not an obstacle.

The conflict-mediation system recommended in this book is based on our experience in organizations as diverse as Fortune 500 companies, federal and state government agencies, nonprofit organizations, hospitals, dental practices, assisted living centers, and other organizations both in the United States and overseas. We believe that the three-stage system described in this book can help healthcare organizations, management, employees, and family members achieve greater alignment and synergy.

Our experience is that while it is not possible to avoid conflict completely, any organization can significantly enhance the ability of managers and employees to reduce unproductive conflict by implementing

standards for guiding conduct and behavior that positively influence the quality of work systems, communication, and relationships among all employees;

a well-understood and accepted process for resolving common conflicts at home and at work; and communication skills and a culture that help sustain a positive work environment.

The good news is that conflict need not be a prescription for poor performance and fractured interpersonal relationships. Applying these three principles above can significantly enhance the ability of your employees and managers to communicate clearly, work constructively, and cooperative to address unproductive conflict on the job. An additional benefit of the conflict-management process recommended in this book is that the skills learned can be applied to your family and in all spheres of your life.

Garry McDaniel, EdD
Leslie Mathew, MD
Mikhail Dernakovski, MD
Alex Batsenko, MD
Gary Stroud, PhD
Siddarth Agrawal, MD

HOW TO USE THIS BOOK

*Why is it that every time I ask for a pair of
hands, they come with a brain attached?*
—Henry Ford

Healthcare organizations can and should learn to deal more effectively with conflict. We also believe that individuals, teams, coworkers, and organizations become stronger and more productive when conflict is transformed into opportunities for cooperation. However, turning conflict into cooperation requires a commitment to the dignity and worth of each individual and a desire to transcend the situation so that a cooperative resolution can be achieved.

This book is based on more than twenty years of collective work experience in the healthcare profession, industry, higher education, government, and nonprofits, and will provide you with the knowledge, skills, and tools to turn everyday conflict into opportunities for enhanced cooperation. An added benefit is that the principles, processes, and skills you will learn can be applied easily in your relationships with family members, friends, and in community groups.

The authors encourage you to use what you learn in this book to try new approaches to communication, address conflict with others, and to reaffirm skills and practices you may already be using effectively. While conflict may occur in many areas of our lives, it does not need to be debilitating. You can transform conflict into cooperation!

Applying this book as an individual:
1. Read the book.
2. Take the self-assessment in chapter one.
3. Reflect upon the skills, knowledge, and tools recommended.
4. Learn the conflict-mediation system.
5. Set aside time each week to work through a specific problem or issue you face in your personal life or at work.
6. Take time to coach others through conflict when the opportunity arises.
7. Be open to being coached by others so that you can continue to enhance your skills.

Applying this book in a group or team:
1. Ask each member of the group or team to read the book to become familiar with the knowledge, skills, and tools.
2. Ask each member to take the self-assessment in chapter one.
3. Work through the tools and activities at the end of each chapter with your colleagues.
4. Conduct a conflict-to-cooperation workshop for all group members. (Train your own staff to conduct this training or use our trained facilitators.)
5. Begin a dialogue regarding how well the group deals with conflict and where you might improve based on what you learned from the book and chapter activities.

6. Seek opportunities to coach each other through conflicts.
7. Periodically review your progress individually and as a group in order to improve.

Applying this book in your organization:
1. Identify the primary sources of unproductive conflict within your organization and what that conflict is costing in terms of quality of care, litigation, stress, employee turnover, etc.
2. Develop or review the vision and goals for your organization.
3. Assess whether you are achieving your organizational mission and goals given your current level of conflict.
4. Critically evaluate the organizational culture and brainstorm how to improve.
5. Provide managers and employees with a copy of this book so they can become familiar with the knowledge, skills, and tools discussed.
6. Send your trainers to our train-the-trainer program or contract with our trained facilitators to customize and conduct the training for your organization.
7. Provide all managers and employees with training on the conflict-to-cooperation model and communication skills.
8. Convene a design team.
9. Work though the implementation process, including training for all managers and employees.
10. Monitor improvements and communicate progress.
11. Review progress periodically and make improvements as needed.

Chapter 1

THE CONFLICT-MEDIATION SYSTEM

> *Culture eats strategy for breakfast.*
> —Peter Drucker

In This Chapter

The focus of chapter one is to help you understand the impact of conflict on the patients, customers, employees, managers, suppliers, and other key stakeholders that comprise or interact with your healthcare organization. You will learn about the cost of unproductive conflict and how individuals typically respond in situations of conflict. You will also learn the primary causes of conflict and the benefits of an effective system for addressing conflicts when they occur. Finally, you will be introduced to the conflict-mediation system that provides organizations and individuals with a method for resolving conflict at the lowest possible level and enhances productivity and respectful interpersonal relationships.

Employees, managers, and administrators in healthcare organizations live and work in a time of increasing pressure and challenges at home and work to do more, with less, and to do so better and faster. Demands for high-quality care, cost control, competition for jobs, and public scrutiny is fierce. Professionals in healthcare organizations often find themselves rushing through life on very little sleep, too much coffee, and under extraordinary pressure to be the perfect employee, caregiver, parent, friend, and associate. As Jim Loehr and Tony Schwartz observe in *The Power of Full Engagement*, "We use words like obsessed, crazed and overwhelmed not to describe insanity, but instead to characterize our daily lives." Does this sound a little like a typical day in your life?

Is it any wonder that under these trying conditions healthcare professionals face increasing levels of stress and conflict at home, work, and in their personal life? Simply put, unproductive conflict is taking a toll on personal well-being, as well as eating away at the health and prosperity of healthcare organizations.

Research in healthcare organizations has consistently found that unproductive conflict and incivility are becoming increasingly commonplace. The resulting negative behaviors and poor communication have led the Joint Commission (2008) to call for zero tolerance to negative behaviors such as bullying, harassment, and incivility, as well as the implementation of a code of conduct for all employees and an organization-wide approach for addressing disruptive behaviors in the workplace. Clearly, healthcare organizations need to do more to ensure a workplace where clear communication, trust, transparency, and the ability to work productively through differences ensures patient safety, and high-quality products and services.

LEADERSHIP and CONFLICT

We believe *everyone* in an organization is a leader and equally responsible for both creating positive conflict and resolving unproductive conflict. This viewpoint supports the current recognition that organizations are not static institutions—they have evolved over time, and each evolution has resulted in increased levels of maturity, consciousness, and complexity. Each stage has required organizations to view themselves and their relationship with those who accomplish the work differently. This may sound a bit paradoxical, so let us take this sentence apart so you understand why we believe this to be true.

Everyone Is a Leader, and Organizations Evolve

First, in today's world, the most innovative companies view everyone as a leader. Of course, this has not always been true. For the great span of human history, leadership was a position bestowed upon the king, pharaoh, queen, tsar, or emperor by a deity. In other words, a god divinely appointed someone as "leader," and everyone else did what they were told—or else! This was true in organizations for thousands of years.

Then, only 200 years ago, the world experienced the industrial revolution and changed from an agriculturally based economy to a factory system. Organizations had to evolve again, and the workplace became increasingly more democratic, with more participative forms of leadership becoming more prevalent. In addition, for the first time in history, in the new industrial work setting, with the right experience or education, individuals could rise through the ranks and take on management and leadership roles. In these organizations, there was still a very strong and clearly defined hierarchy, but "followers" were given more autonomy in how to accomplish directives from management.

With the advent of the "information age," organizations began to realize that to be nimble, competitive, and innovative, they needed to push "empowerment" throughout the organization. This meant giving employees even more room to grow, develop, and give "bottom-up" input into policies, processes, and work conditions. In the past twenty years, more and more innovative companies have begun to place a strong emphasis on vision and values. However, you have probably noticed that while it is easy for an organization to create and articulate a vision and values, attaining consistency between what is said and what is done is very difficult. Note that while they are more participative, "information-age" organizations are still top-down hierarchies where senior administrators and highly educated professionals wield the greatest power and control. So, while these organizations are more participative, there is frequently a large gap between what the company *says it values*, and a company *culture* that still allows bullying, incivility, disrespect, hazing, and harassment to exist. The result is probably what you are seeing in your organization right now: low morale, high turnover, lack of teamwork, decreased quality, increased mistakes, poor communication, unproductive conflict, and an increase in sick leave and grievances.

Notice in the three stages presented above, over time organizations found it necessary to change the way they were organized and how they viewed employees. Organizations evolved from absolute monarchies to the machine-age view that people could advance in their role, to the information age where teamwork and participation are valued. As each evolution occurred, organizations became *vastly* more productive, and better places to work.

Despite these advances, people sense that the way organizations are operated and managed today is not working. According to the Gallup organization, only 34 percent of workers in the United States and 13 percent of employees and managers worldwide come to work feeling enthusiastic, involved in, and committed to their workplace. This means that somewhere between 66 percent and 87 percent of your workforce is showing up to work every day to either go through the motions of doing their job, or actively drain the productivity, quality, and vitality from the organization. The good news is that plenty of organizations have developed and implemented effective cultures for addressing unproductive conflict. If they can do it, so can you.

Take a minute to consider what the most innovative companies are doing that is different from what most other companies are doing. These innovative organizations have an intense focus on establishing cultures in which all employees can align their professional and life purpose with that of the organization. They focus on creating safe, collaborative, respectful work environments where everyone is a leader who has the skills to do their job and share their opinion and perspective. Today's organizations recognize that hiring talented people who can align behind and support the purpose and values of the organization is the key to success. So, if your organization is still struggling with reducing the gap between the values and quality of care, products, or services you say is important, and an environment where people have learned to "just do what they are told," your organization is being left behind. It is time to evolve.

We hope that the individuals in your organization with lofty titles and salaries are also effective leaders, but today's employees are keenly aware that titles and big salaries do not mean a person is a good leader. Nor do titles and salaries ensure effective communication, teamwork, and collaboration. Truly great leaders are able to influence themselves and others to achieve positive outcomes in an ethical manner. This means *anyone* in an organization can be a model of effective leadership since all employees are responsible and accountable not just for their own work but also for working with others to serve the larger purpose of the organization and ensure patient safety.

Leaders Create Conflict through Change

Second, leaders create conflict by introducing change. Whether the change is building a new hospital, implementing a new surgical technique, hiring new staff, learning something new, or introducing a new drug, service, laboratory technique, or a new software system, you are asking people to change what they are doing. Even when a change is something everyone agrees is necessary, people still have to stop doing what they were doing and do something new. This is true on an organizational level and at the individual level. For example, at the individual level, if you start a new job, decide to lose weight, pursue additional education, or even go on a trip, you introduce change and conflict into your life and the lives of others.

Leaders Help Others Navigate through Conflict

Third, effective leaders do not create conflict (introduce change) and then walk away hoping that someone else will deal with the challenges or chaos that follows. Effective leaders help others to recognize the need *for* change and then work collaboratively *with* others to work *through* the conflict that inevitably follows. That means effective leaders do not pretend they cannot see conflict, avoid conflict, or push the responsibility for resolving conflict off on others. (At best, this is ignorance, dereliction of duty, or just plain cowardice.) Senior leaders in innovative companies also recognize that they are not the only source of insight and information in the world. By listening to all employees with respect and empathy, relationships are strengthened, greater insight is gained, and growth is encouraged.

Great Leaders Act Ethically

Think for a minute about the difference between the leadership of Adolph Hitler and Mohandas Gandhi. While both meet the guidelines described above, there is a *huge* difference in the outcomes each pursued, and the ethics (or lack thereof) they practiced. Therefore, the fourth element of our view of leadership is that great leaders work with others to achieve *positive outcomes that are ethical*. This means the outcomes achieved must be good for everyone and in accordance with the organization's positive values, principles, codes of conduct, ethical standards, and laws. Positive, ethical leadership does not mean one person does what is good for themselves at the expense of others. It does mean that you create a culture and provide people the skills where opportunities and problems are discussed openly and respectfully.

Because leaders introduce change, which causes conflict, and all employees are leaders, everyone should recognize that conflict and change are a natural part of work and life. The key challenge organizations face is the *will and commitment* to develop a culture of trust where all employees have the skills and desire to appreciate each other, communicate effectively, problem-solve, and work collaboratively to reach the best outcomes.

PRODUCTIVE vs. UNPRODUCTIVE CONFLICT

We define *productive conflict* as an open exchange of differing ideas in which the people involved feel heard, respected, and unafraid to voice their opinions to reach the most effective positive outcome. Productive conflict is valuable to friends, family, coworkers, suppliers, and patients because it builds trust, respect, and makes us more productive and creative when interacting with each other. Productive conflict drives successful healthcare organizations forward, leads to creative, innovative ideas and solutions, and it helps enhance relationships by allowing everyone to respectfully confront each other so that we all improve in a constructive way and without insults and bruised egos.

Unproductive conflict, as you have no doubt experienced personally, can be very destructive. Unproductive conflict can take the form of belittling or abusive behavior, favoritism, intentional damage to organizational resources, theft, harassment, bullying, withholding information, and even workplace violence. A key characteristic of unproductive conflict is that often the "conflict" is addressed superficially, and the real or substantive driving forces or emotions behind the conflict or difference of opinion are never really surfaced or resolved. This means the conflict never really goes away and continues to fester. The result of unproductive conflict is that it tears down relationships, creates barriers and silos between people, and feeds upon itself to make things even worse. Unproductive conflict is what we all hate about conflict in the first place.

THE COST of UNPRODUCTIVE CONFLICT

When people in healthcare organizations work productively to address and resolve conflict, the benefit is greater trust, high morale, a widespread commitment to providing quality care, services, and products, and enhanced working relationships. On the flip side, the inability to work through conflict causes great stress among employees and management that costs organizations time, money, and ill will not only internally, but also with patients, suppliers, regulators, and the public. In many cases, unproductive conflict at work goes home with a person and affects those whom they love and even one's health.

For example, in one study, American employees reported spending 2.8 hours per week dealing with conflict, amounting to approximately $359 billion in paid hours, or the equivalent of 385 million working days in the country as a whole. Further, 25 percent of employees said that avoiding conflict led to sickness or absence from work, and nearly 10 percent reported that workplace conflict led to project failure (Menon and Thompson 2018). In addition, companies spend hundreds of millions of dollars on conflict-management training, team building, and interpersonal skills; but these expenditures are not being translated into effective, collaborative work. What happens is that employees go to these training programs and say, "That would be great if I could use these skills where I work." Then they return to a work environment and culture that does not support the new behaviors.

Unproductive conflict is also unnecessarily commonplace in most healthcare environments. Research on healthcare workplaces consistently documents a lack of civility, respect, and care. For example, when asked if she experienced a workplace where unproductive conflict occurred, a labor and delivery nurse said, "Are you kidding? I experience it every day, and I see conflict sucking the life out our ability to work together and serve patients across the department. Management and human resources act as if conflict does not exist until something blows up!"

Let's look at an all-too-familiar example from the healthcare profession. In a small, regional hospital, a registered nurse (RN) filed a complaint with human resources regarding treatment she received from the head nurse. The RN reported that over a six-month period, tensions between her and the head nurse escalated to the point the RN felt she was working in a hostile environment. The RN claimed that the head nurse was overly critical, unfair in scheduling, and had publicly ridiculed her on several occasions. As a result, she and the head nurse were not communicating, and information regarding patient care was not being shared consistently or as thoroughly as needed. The RN also observed that other staff in the unit felt the same way, but were afraid to say anything for fear of reprisal.

The head nurse responded that she and the RN simply had different work styles. In addition, as the head nurse, she felt it was her prerogative to schedule staff as she saw fit and that it was her responsibility to provide corrective communications when she saw something occurring that could affect patient care.

Because of the conflict, the RN began to accumulate a significant amount of sick time that was attributed to work-related stress. Other employees in the unit also spent an unnecessary amount of time discussing the situation, with some employees taking the side of the RN and some the side of the head nurse.

An investigation into the situation identified a number of issues that contributed to the conflict between these two individuals, including
- a lack of communication skills among all unit staff
- no conflict-management skills training
- infrequent or incomplete communication between the head nurse and other staff

- unnecessary time spent by all employees on negative gossip
- generational differences in how employees perceived their work practices, roles, and responsibilities

The investigation found that due to the unresolved conflict, the head nurse, RN, and other unit staff were providing poor service to patients and placing the hospital in jeopardy of mistakes or litigation.

This is clearly an example of how unproductive conflict can exacerbate problems and become a serious obstruction to quality care. You have probably experienced poor service or outcomes such as this in your healthcare organization, or in hotels, retail stores, restaurants, gas stations, repair shops, and countless other business and government offices across the country. The result is the same: conflict gets in the way of the primary reason for the organization's very existence *and* the purpose of the employee's job—serving the customer.

Many people are simply not aware of the impact unproductive conflict can have on the organization, customers, and on people. Research indicates that the cost of conflict may fall into one or more of the following categories:

- *Direct Costs* include litigation expenses for attorney fees, expert witnesses, trial, appeals, and settlements.
- *Productivity Costs* include the value of lost time, errors, wasted resources, loss of intellectual property, employee turnover, and retraining.
- *Opportunity Costs* include what those involved would otherwise have been producing if they were not embroiled in conflict. This might take the form of failure to capitalize on new ideas, missed sales, poor service that translates into a lost customer, etc.
- *Continuity Costs* include the loss of existing relationships among one's network, customers, associates, vendors, suppliers, manufacturers, and friends.
- *Emotional Costs* include the personal turmoil and stress we feel when dealing with situations of conflict.

The effect of these costs is not always immediately apparent. In the example of the RN and head nurse, the impact of their conflict and poor communication could have been a medical mistake that led to litigation. The RN (or another employee) could have decided to leave, at which time the organization would have had to incur recruiting and training expenses to find a replacement. Because the two individuals were not communicating fully, the opportunity to demonstrate excellent patient care and a positive health environment was missed. Very possibly, patients might have gone home to complain to workmates, friends, and family members about the poor quality of care provided by the hospital. Finally, these two individuals and other unit staff experienced stress and turmoil due to the ongoing, negative situation.

Let's look at another example.

Bright Futures Medical Center was a large hospital in a metropolitan community that was struggling with attracting and retaining talented employees and maintaining its reputation as a provider of quality healthcare. Internal satisfaction surveys over several years provided consistent data that employees at all levels with Bright Futures felt that one of the major solutions for overcoming this stagnation was to significantly improve the quality of management and leadership skills. Mary, a talented professional with a strong record of accomplishment for developing leadership programs, was hired to design and implement a comprehensive leadership-development process for the hospital. During interviews and upon her acceptance of the job, she was given repeated assurances that senior management was committed to providing the necessary support and resources required to ensure this effort was successful.

During the first few months, Mary reviewed the satisfaction-survey data, benchmarked leadership-development programs at other highly regarded healthcare institutions, and developed a comprehensive plan for providing effective management and leadership development at the executive, middle, and first-line manager levels. Mary presented the plan to her manager, and was told that he would present it "up the ladder." Two months went by during which he said the plan was "still under review." He declined her offer to personally present and explain the plan to higher-level executives. After four months of little feedback, Mary's manager said upper management thought the proposal was a little too costly, although it had been within the budget originally allocated. As a result, she was asked to revise and resubmit the development plan. She did so, and once again, two more months elapsed with little feedback.

However, during this period, Mary was able to meet informally with several of the senior executives and discuss her proposals for the leadership-development plan. These meetings led to three very important insights. First, Mary was surprised to find that none of the executives accepted the validity of the original employee-survey data regarding the need for more effective leadership. Rather, each executive shared a common view that "employees didn't know what they were talking about," the effectiveness of their personal leadership was beyond question, and any problem of poor management and leadership skills must lie at the middle and first-line manager level. Second, Mary learned that few, if any, executives even felt that leadership training was needed. One executive seemed to speak for the rest when he observed, "We don't need leadership training! I'm the leader of my division. If my employees want to learn about leadership, they should just watch me!" Finally, Mary learned that the majority of employees did not feel that Bright Futures had successfully implemented a successful cultural-change effort in the past five years. This was reinforced from her interactions with senior executives who observed that any people-oriented change efforts were "soft," "a waste of time," and "not bottom-line driven."

Mary was directed to modify her plan a third time to focus on development for only middle and first-line managers. Dutifully, Mary revised and resubmitted her plan for these two groups. Again, months passed in which there was little communication regarding the revised plan. Ultimately, her manager informed her that the "higher-ups" still viewed the plan as too costly and directed her to cut out any development for middle management; only first-line managers would now receive training.

In subsequent meetings with her manager, Mary reminded him of the validity of the survey data, the promises of support made by the executives, and the difference a well-designed management and leadership-training program would make to the company. Her manager became increasingly agitated, stressing that Mary should "not make waves," "just do what you're told," "be glad you have a job," etc. Then, to Mary's astonishment, he asked her to write articles for the local newspaper and to make conference presentations suggesting that Bright Futures Medical Center was developing a "world-class" leadership-development program for all management levels.

Finally, she had enough. Mary felt that she had wasted over a year in the job without seeing any substantive support or producing a single workshop to address the management and leadership needs of Bright Futures Medical Center. Disillusioned, she left the company to establish a comprehensive leadership program with a manufacturing company in the city. Over the next year, Bright Futures Medical Center saw a continuing trend of above-average turnover among key professional positions, their absenteeism rate increased by 20 percent, and their number of sick days taken doubled.

The conflict described in this case centers around executive management's unwillingness to look critically at its own behavior and opportunities for improvement. In completing the satisfaction survey, employees expressed their view that the lack of cohesive, strategic leadership was keeping Bright Futures Medical Center from attaining the level of quality care and workplace satisfaction that was possible. Instead of considering this data in a thoughtful manner, Bright Future's executive management became defensive and pronounced that the employees did not know what they were talking about and that their executive leadership skills were beyond question.

So, what were the costs? At a minimum, the direct costs to Bright Futures Medical Center were the wasted salary and benefits to Mary for over one year. This would include the costs incurred to interview, recruit, relocate, and train Mary. Productivity costs were lost as Mary was not able to provide any substantive contribution to Bright Futures Medical Center over the period of her employment. Opportunity costs incurred included the missed improvements in productivity, efficiency, and employee morale that might have been attained had the leadership skills of the management and executive staff been improved.

In addition, Bright Futures Medical Center had an opportunity to demonstrate to employees that the organization truly listened to the opinions expressed in employee-satisfaction surveys. By belittling and ignoring their input, executives simply enhanced a widespread perception among employees that "our opinions don't matter." Continuity costs were impacted when Mary left the hospital. When Mary left, the relationships that she had established with the organization for supporting the management and leadership-development program were lost. The emotional cost to Bright Futures Medical Center was staggering. Employee confidence in their immediate management and executive leadership declined. Finally, Mary left the company feeling embittered at what she felt had been a "total waste of my time."

The lesson from the case of Bright Futures Medical Center is that potentially hundreds of thousands of dollars of time, effort, and productivity were wasted due to the inability of executive management to recognize and work through a conflict. Executives became entrenched in defending their personal egos instead of honestly considering consistent internal and external data suggesting their leadership skills be improved. At the very least, Bright Futures Medical Center lost a great employee, created additional mistrust between management and employees, and shortchanged the community of people needing care—all because they could not bear to look critically at their own contribution to the problem.

While one might hope that unproductive conflict is not apparent to patients or customers, this is rarely the case. Consider the following narrative shared by a husband and wife during a hospital stay that should have been a joyous occasion.

"Earlier this year, my wife and I welcomed our twins into the world. Because of some complications, my wife and the twins needed to be in the hospital for six days. During this period, we were exposed to a variety of healthcare providers and departments and witnessed an organization and employees who were clearly at odds with each other over policy, protocol, and philosophy of care.

"Some of the issues were procedural, with different staff trying to carry out protocols that were in contrast with what other staff were doing. More troublesome was the constant need to update the hospital physicians and other caregivers on what care had been already been delivered and ordered previously. We found that while each department tracked well from one shift to the next, departments that relied on information from another department experienced significant gaps or delays.

"The issue was not technical, since the hospital seemed to have a fully functioning, up-to-date computer system to do this. Instead, the information simply did not flow from one person to the next, and it fell upon us—the patients—to keep the staff informed. More than once one caregiver would want to provide a treatment one way, and another caregiver would say, 'No, that is not how it is done in our area,' and then the two would argue about it in front of us. This disagreement caused us to seriously question the competence of everyone—particularly when the safety of our infant twins was at stake!"

In *The Magic of Conflict,* Thomas Crum shares the good news that conflict such as was experienced in these cases does not have to be so costly. Rather, Crum observes that we can choose to view conflict as a natural part of life. The physical forces and changing weather patterns of the world around us are the result of the natural conflicts that shape the environment. For example, it is the conflict, or irritation, within an oyster that creates a pearl. It is the conflict between water and land that creates beaches, canyons, and scenic mountain valleys. Crum notes that conflict is a gift of energy in which neither side loses. Rather, productive conflict is the natural outgrowth of change, of improvement, or movement away from the status quo.

Traditionally, conflict is defined as a situation in which "the ideas, interests or behavior of two or more individuals or groups clash." Nothing in this definition suggests conflict must be unproductive. You may want to accomplish a task in one way, and I may want to accomplish that task in a different way. It is often the case that because of our different perspectives, we come up with an even better solution than we would have independently.

RESPONDING to CONFLICT

There are at least five different ways people respond when presented with a conflict (Figure 1). Each method has its own advantages and disadvantages depending on the individuals involved, circumstances, values, and cultural, political, and religious factors. In other words, there is no one best conflict style in all situations; rather, one style may be appropriate for one situation and inappropriate for another. Each method results in a different combination of win-lose outcomes. In this section, you will learn how to distinguish one style from another, the advantages and disadvantages of each, and when it is appropriate to use one style over another.

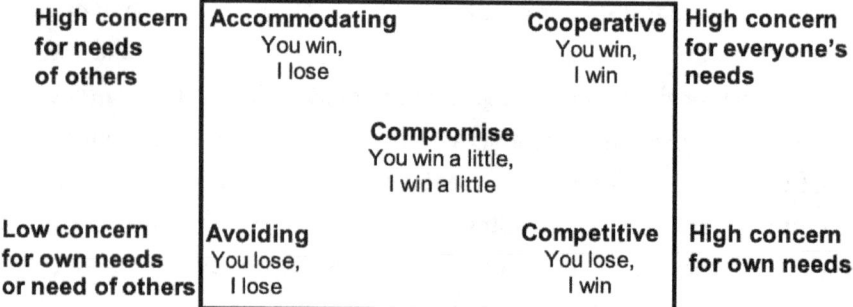

Figure 1: Conflict-Management Styles

Method One: Avoidance

The first method for dealing with conflict is avoidance. An individual who avoids conflict attempts to ignore the conflict nonverbally or emotionally. Rather than face it openly, they are unassertive and uncooperative. By minimizing a problem, changing the subject, joking about a conflict, or putting the problem off, people avoid the issue in question. This creates a lose-lose situation.

The advantage of the avoiding style is that it may help maintain relationships that could be damaged by surfacing the conflict. The disadvantage of this style is that conflicts do not get resolved. Let's face it, not everyone likes conflict, and some people avoid any conflict situation at all costs. But if an individual continually relies on avoiding conflict, others tend to take advantage of them, and the individual never achieves their own goals. When a healthcare organization, its management, or employees avoid conflict, they run the risk that the conflict will escalate and any challenges between groups or individuals will be exacerbated. In fact, a primary complaint by employees is that their manager (and often human resources) will not address conflict when it occurs; rather, that management pretends not to "see" the conflict, provides only superficial efforts to respond to the conflict, or avoids conflict altogether. In some cases, employees report that if they approach management or human resources with a complaint or grievance, they are then perceived as the "problem" or not a "team player." The unspoken message to all employees becomes one of "we avoid conflict in this organization and hope it goes away."

Method Two: Accommodation

A second method of responding to conflict is accommodation or "giving in." When one relies on the accommodating style, one is being unassertive by attempting to satisfy the other party but neglecting their own needs. This creates a win-lose situation. The accommodating style is different from the avoiding style. For example, when one avoids conflict, they do not have to do anything that they do not want to do. When one person accommodates someone else, they are giving in to the other individual.

The advantage of the accommodating style is that relationships are maintained by going along with the other person. The disadvantage is that "giving in" may be counterproductive.

The person who is "giving in" may actually have a better idea or solution. As with the avoiding style, when individuals overuse the accommodating style, they tend to get taken advantage of. The accommodating style is appropriate to use when

- you enjoy being a follower
- the issue or problem is not important to you but is to the other party
- it is important to maintain the relationship
- the time needed to resolve the conflict is limited

Method Three: Compromise

The third method is to compromise—or "You give half and I give half." When utilizing this style, an individual attempts to resolve the conflict through assertive, give-and-take negotiations. This leads to an "I win some, you win some" or "I give a little, and you give a little" outcome. The advantage of the compromising style is that it can be effective for resolving a conflict relatively quickly, and working relationships are maintained. The disadvantage is that by compromising, both parties may be giving up something that they really need or want. This can lead to dissatisfaction and may ultimately undermine the agreed-upon solution. It is appropriate to use the compromising style when

- the issues are complex and there are no simple, clear solutions
- both parties have equal power and are interested in different solutions
- time is short
- a solution will only be temporary

Method Four: Competing

In the competitive approach, the person with the most power in terms of time, money, resources, position, or communication style negotiates from a "I win, you lose" point of view. An individual relying on this style is generally more aggressive, uncooperative, and does what they can to get the results they desire at the expense of others. They may use authority, threats, and intimidation to get their desired solution, or in group situations they may call for majority voting if they think they can win. Individuals who gravitate to the competitive style like to deal with people who are avoiders and accommodators because it is much easier to "run all over them."

The advantage of the competitive style is that sometimes you can reach decisions in a short amount of time. This can be helpful when the competitive individual is correct, but this method often results in defensiveness and leads others to dig in their heels, thereby bringing the resolution of a conflict to a halt. Those people who continually wind up on the losing end of a conflict situation will generally begin to respond through overt or passive aggression, withholding information or effort, sabotage, or otherwise "getting back" at the individual who "won." A constant reliance on the competitive style can also lead to what the Gallup Organization terms "disengagement" by employees.

Method Five: Cooperation

The final approach people use when dealing with situations involving conflict is to cooperate. The cooperative method is preferable for organizations and groups that need a method for managing conflict that respects the needs of others and enables everyone to discuss their own needs and wants. (Current research clearly indicates that this is the direction the most innovative organizations are already headed. See Frederic Laloux's book, *Reinventing Organizations*, for a thorough explanation of this trend.)

Cooperative decision-making assumes that the parties involved share a similar goal to achieve a mutually satisfactory or "win-win" solution, and are fully capable of doing so. Cooperative decision-making does not mean that all group members have to be best friends or that they will always agree with each other, but does assume that the parties involved can create enough options, choices, or solutions for each side to find satisfactory agreement.

While avoiders and accommodators are more concerned about the needs of *others*, and competitors are concerned about their *own* needs, parties relying on the cooperative approach are genuinely interested in finding the best solution to a problem that is satisfactory to all participants. Unlike the competitor, the cooperative individual is willing and often eager to change his or her opinion or approach if a better solution is introduced. In addition, while collaborating can be based on withholding information, the cooperative style is based on open, honest, transparent communication.

The advantage of the cooperative style is that it tends to achieve the best solutions because all of the people involved are honestly and openly trying to reach the best possible result. The disadvantage of this approach is that it takes time and skill to implement effectively. Even if more time and skill is spent to reach a solution that everyone

fully supports, that is a lot better than reaching a solution that most people disagree with and might try to sabotage. It is appropriate to use the cooperative style when
- you are dealing with an important problem that requires the best solution
- people are willing to place the group goal over self-interest
- maintaining relationships is important
- time is available

It is possible to apply more than one of these approaches at once. In the example of Bright Futures Medical Center, the executives relied on their position of power to *avoid* validating data that pointed to a connection between their leadership ability and institutional challenges. Mary went from trying to *cooperate* with her manager and executives to provide a truly world-class program, to *compromising* on a process simply for first-line management. Ultimately, when she saw that there was no support for a solution in which she truly believed, she simply "gave up" and withdrew from the organization.

Slaikeu and Hasson, two researchers in the area of conflict management, note that each of these methods of responding to conflict is appropriate for different circumstances, and have constructive and destructive forms. For example, in one situation, you may not have a real interest in an issue and choose to avoid responding to a conflict because of other higher priorities. This would be an example of a constructive response to a conflict. On the other hand, if you avoid a conflict which is causing stress, or in which you have a clear stake, this would be an example of a destructive response to a conflict. Again, when the executives at Bright Futures Medical Center avoided looking critically at how their lack of leadership skills influenced business operations and employee morale, they exhibited an unproductive response to dealing with conflict that cost tens of millions of dollars.

We each have our own way of dealing with conflict. The techniques we choose to rely upon most frequently are based on many variables, such as our basic underlying temperament, our personality, our environment, and where we are in our professional career. At the end of this chapter, you will find a Conflict-Management Style Survey that was adapted from *How to Manage Conflict* by Peg Pickering. By taking this short survey, you will learn which style or styles you tend to gravitate toward. Remember that none of these strategies is superior in and of itself. How effective they are depends on the context in which they are used.

CAUSES of UNPRODUCTIVE CONFLICT

At work and in our personal lives, we live at a frantic pace. You may be putting in eight to ten hours a day at work trying to balance pressing daily tasks with the long-term growth, planning, and development needed for personal and organizational success. You then add on a few more hours of commute time, trips to the grocery store, taking kids to band or soccer practice, and rushing to complete errands—all in the same day. With all of these pressures, it is no wonder that we have conflicts at home, with other drivers on the highway, within our work units, across divisions, and throughout companies.

There are three main reasons organizations suffer the effects of unproductive conflict (Figure 2).

Figure 2 : Conflict-Mediation System

First, management and employees often do not share, practice, and hold each other accountable to *standards for guiding behavior and conduct*. For example, in our training and consulting practice, we occasionally find that executives, managers, and employees *say* they value respecting and listening to others, diversity of opinion, and so on, but in practice they behave in ways that are interpreted as being dishonest, disrespectful, uncivil, harassing, adversarial, authoritarian, or even unethical.

Second, we frequently find that managers and employees lack a *common process for resolving conflicts* when they occur. It is important to have a process that all people involved understand and apply to enable everyone to share ideas, opinions, needs, goals, and action strategies safely. This process should encourage each person to work collaboratively with others to keep the higher purpose, goals, and standards of the organization in mind so that a solution is achieved that is truly best for everyone involved.

Third, it is important to have the *skills to communicate effectively*, and not violate the dignity and worth of others. When all employees have effective communications skills, they are able to communicate with each other in ways that ensure understanding, build trust, and enhance relationships. This means having the skill to truly listen, avoid making assumptions, and speak to others in ways that are not belittling or disrespectful.

As Figure 2 above illustrates, these three factors are interdependent; a change in one affects the other two. In our experience, all three must be present for people to address conflict effectively and are important elements in the development of a positive workplace culture. To understand how these three factors work within an organization, consider the following scenario:

Imagine that you are watching a professional baseball team. Your favorite team is in the field, there are no runners on base, and the opposing team's batter hits a ground ball directly to the shortstop. Instead of throwing the ball to first base to get the runner out, the shortstop simply tosses the ball back to the pitcher, and the runner is able to get on base safely.

The team manager calls a quick "time out" and runs onto the field to have a discussion with the pitcher, shortstop, and first baseman. The team manager begins by asking the shortstop why he did not throw the ball to the first baseman to get the runner out.

"Well," the shortstop replies, "yesterday the first baseman and I had an argument, and I'm not going to throw the ball to him again until he apologizes. Not only that, sometimes he comes to practice late, and thinks his job on first base is more important than mine."

Do you feel this is a valid response? How would you react if you were the team manager? How do you think the other players on the team would feel? What must the fans be thinking? Wouldn't you be angry, disappointed, and incredulous that a professional baseball player would resort to such a juvenile way of thinking during a game? Most people would feel completely justified in saying to the shortstop, "I don't care which team member you are angry at; your job is to help us win the game!"

Why is it that we seldom see this level of petty behavior on *any* professional sports team? We believe it is because professional athletes consciously or unconsciously understand and practice the three elements of the conflict-mediation system and work within a culture that supports and encourages effective teamwork and success.

First, professional athletes are committed to standards that guide their behavior and conduct and the behavior and conduct of every other player on the field. These standards include the rules of the game, roles and responsibilities, penalties for playing poorly (fines, loss of employment or endorsements, ostracism by other team members, bad press, etc.) and rewards for playing well (salary, bonuses, fan adoration, endorsements, and so on). Professional athletes understand that if they are to win, they must play as a team. This means valuing team play and each other's skills over personal egos.

Second, they have a strong and well-understood process by which they play the game. This process includes the systematic steps to play the game. For example, in football, the process of play includes a coin toss, kickoff, kick return, downs, defense, and extra point attempts. The process of play is logical and fair. A team does not try an extra point, kick off, and then have the coin toss. This is also true for other sports.

Finally, professional athletes not only work hard to develop their skills, but they also practice continually and receive constant coaching to enhance their ability to play the game. Professional athletes do not practice once at the beginning of the season and simply play "real" games the remainder of the year. They practice the same basic skills, review strategies, and receive individualized improvement coaching on a daily basis throughout the year. Most companies send employees to training and assume that whatever the topic was, the employee now is an expert for life!

Now, keep the baseball game in mind as you read the next scenario taken from a real incident.

Wendy Brown is the operations manager for Children's Hospital. One day, Wendy receives a phone call from the hospital administrator, who tells Wendy that he is not happy with the cleanliness of the complex. The administrator advises Wendy that she needs to have a talk with her people before the day is out, and he wants to see immediate improvement.

Anxious to find the underlying cause of this problem, Wendy assures the administrator that she will personally investigate the problem and see that it is corrected. She hurries down to the floor to talk to those cleaning the building. When she arrives, the evening shift change is taking place.

As Wendy waits for the shift change to be completed, she notices members of the first shift are not making any effort to communicate what areas of the building need extra attention. Wendy knows it is vital that the incoming shift understands which floors are on rotation to be polished that night or where extra cleaning is needed.

Wendy stops the outgoing shift supervisor and asks why his departing shift is not ensuring that the incoming shift members completely understand the maintenance schedule.

"Oh," the supervisor replies. "A couple of weeks ago, I was trying to explain a potential problem at our shift-change meeting. The supervisor of the second shift didn't agree and made it look like I didn't know what I was talking about in front of everyone. She is such a big 'know-it-all,' and made me look like an idiot. Worse, no one even said a thing to her or stuck up for me. You can bet I'm not going to bring that problem up again!"

"But certainly," Wendy answered, "you realize that a poor pass-down process must mean that over the past few weeks the quality of the floors and other building maintenance has been slipping and is below our requirements?"

"Of course," he says. "But I am not going to get my tail chewed off whenever I try to point out a potential problem. Plus, once she hears from you, it will prove I was right, and she was wrong!"

How would you react if you were Wendy? The hospital administrator has called you on the carpet because of the way the complex is looking. Wouldn't you be angry and disappointed? Wouldn't you feel justified in saying, "I don't care which other employee you are angry at. You're paid to produce high-quality work!" Incidentally, when we present this scenario at workshops, we very frequently have participants laugh, smile, ruefully shake their heads, and observe, "That happens here all the time!"

The key question you should consider is how is the situation with the nurse and head nurse and Bright Futures Medical Center at the beginning of this chapter or with Wendy and her colleagues at Children's Hospital any different than a professional baseball team? Aren't the employees of these healthcare organizations paid professionals? Aren't they *supposed* to be working together for the benefit of the rest of the group? Isn't patient care, customer service, high quality, reducing mistakes, and working as a team the purpose or desired outcome for both organizations?

The answer is yes, the employees in the two healthcare organizations should be working together to resolve conflicts productively. But—and this is a HUGE but—the difference is that on the playing field, unproductive conflict is apparent to *everyone*. It is apparent because everyone, including players, fans, and coaches, all understand the standards that guide behavior and conduct, the process of the game, and the skills required of the players so well that any deviation from the standard of excellence is abundantly clear. Further, the players and coaches all hold each other accountable for performing at their best all of the time, not just some of the time. Those sports organizations that do not put their entire focus on ensuring these three elements are enacted at the highest level are generally playing at the bottom of their league.

We have found that well-intentioned healthcare organizations frequently
- lack or fail to follow clear standards for guiding behavior and conduct with each other
- do not have a process by which they can make decisions, resolve problems, and address conflicts
- lack skills needed to communicate effectively with each other and which are practiced regularly

As a result, these organizations routinely ignore and/or fail to deal with unproductive conflict until these conflicts reach crisis proportions.

THE VALUE of COOPERATION

Organizations rely on employees to work interdependently because it is simply good business. When people work well together, patient care, customer service, operations, and delivery of services are significantly enhanced. Studies conducted by Dr. Michael Beyerlein, the former executive director for the Center for Collaborative Organizations, found that groups that work collaboratively are more effective in assisting organizations to
- improve service delivery
- meet or exceed customer needs
- introduce improvements and/or innovations
- integrate and streamline organizational structures, systems, and processes
- design, develop, and produce products
- enhance employee morale and retention
- speed new-employee orientation and training
- reduce costs and inventory while increasing service quality

Where group collaboration is lacking or inefficient, service delivery declines, customer or patient needs are not met, improvements or innovations lag, and maintaining the status quo becomes the norm as product-cycle times suffer. Instead of increased profits and job security, profits fall and people worry about the long-term safety of their jobs.

In these and similar studies, organizations and group members also identified sources that not only sap the efficiency and effectiveness of organizational work environments, but also cause great stress among employees and management.

Sources of conflict include situations in which employees

- consistently arrive to work late, take breaks early, and come back from breaks late
- avoid helping orient or train other employees
- show little interest in learning new skills or taking on new responsibilities
- intentionally belittle, put down, bully, or tease other employees
- fail to clearly communicate information, needs, or expectations
- "punch the clock" and go home, or never stay late when needed
- refuse to share information, tools, or supplies with others
- form cliques that side against other employees or work units

Employees often report that a great deal of the conflict they experience is related to poor management. Sources of conflict reported by employees include managers who

- practice favoritism
- lack integrity and honesty
- worry about themselves more than employees or the institution
- fail to recognize and reward employee contributions
- fail to support or provide opportunities for employee growth and development
- fail to provide direction or clearly communicate expectations
- have "retired on the job" and fail to initiate or support positive change
- provide inconsistent or inadequate communication
- "talk the talk" but do not "walk the walk"
- fail to address conflict

- apply one standard of behavior or ethics to employees and another to management

If unproductive conflict has such negative consequences, why do we expect so much from professional athletes, and so little from managers and employees in organizations? After all, like professional athletes, managers and employees are paid and trained to apply interpersonal skills, to work effectively within the organizational process, and to be committed to the organization.

As suggested earlier, we believe management and employees fail to work with each other and deal with conflict effectively because they lack a system for doing so. If management and employees do not share standards of conduct and behavior, have no process for addressing problems and conflicts, and lack effective communications skills, why should we not expect a high level of discord?

THE CONFLICT-MEDIATION SYSTEM

The conflict-mediation system presented in this book provides healthcare organizations with a method for resolving the conflicts that act as barriers to patient care and organizational efficiency, and that cause employees stress and frustration. When fully implemented, this system will also encourage management and employees to recognize and resolve conflicts productively at the lowest possible organizational level.

The next chapter will focus on explaining how standards of conduct and behavior are crucial for building trust, cooperation, and effective interpersonal relationships. These standards are often identified as codes of conduct, principles, or values that should guide how business is conducted, how people treat each other, and the ethical and legal rules by which they operate. These standards—and whether they are truly embraced or simply given lip service—are crucial to creating the culture of the organization.

The conflict-mediation process provides managers and employees with a common approach for addressing problems, challenges, and conflicts when they occur. This process provides all involved with a common language and model for sharing ideas, opinions, needs, and goals. This process is described in chapter three.

Finally, management and employees also need the skills to communicate effectively with each other. Communication is vital to interpersonal and organizational relationships; it is how work ultimately is done. Managers and employees must be able to communicate in ways that promote understanding and relationships, and help achieve organizational goals. If people communicate in ways that cause defensiveness, relationships sour, productivity declines, and service is eroded. Communication skills are discussed in chapter four.

Together, these three elements comprise a holistic system. Eliminating, minimizing, or adapting one element of the system changes the nature of the results you can expect. For example, if a healthcare organization has effective communication skills and a process for mediating conflicts, but management or other professionals behave in ways that are unethical, disrespectful, bullying, lacking integrity, or dishonest, employees will lack trust and a cooperative spirit. If an organization has standards that guide behavior and conduct and a process for mediating conflicts, but employees lack the skills to communicate effectively with each other, miscommunication will occur, mistakes will be made, and morale will suffer. If an organization has standards of behavior and conduct and effective communication skills, but lacks a process for resolving conflicts, then management and employees will approach conflicts and challenges without a common language or framework for logically addressing those conflicts. Assumptions and expectations may not be identified, and those involved may find themselves leaping from identifying the conflict to a "solution" that is short lived.

Research suggests that the relationship between an employee and his or her manager is critical to both morale and productivity. The role of effective management is to provide clear direction, to create a work environment that is positive and supportive, to promote growth and development, and to achieve progress or results. To accomplish this role, managers must deal effectively with conflicts. In chapter five, you will learn how to coach coworkers, peers, employees, and others through conflict.

Managers and employees often ask how they can implement this system with their organization. Their concern is often that they are not beginning with a clean record. Rather, they are aware of a history of mistrust, abuse, or confrontation between management and employees. They often describe situations where employees and management have demonstrated long-standing interpersonal rivalries and grievances against each other. Further, work units may also have deeply entrenched silos with powerful egos to overcome. In chapter six, you will learn how to plan and implement the conflict-mediation system within your organization and address these challenges in a positive manner.

Finally, most of us have full lives outside of work. In chapter seven, you will learn how to apply the conflict-mediation system at home and other settings outside of the workplace. Let's get started!

The Least You Need To Remember

- Conflict has a price. Productive conflict pays off in better quality, service, and relationships.
- There are five methods for responding to conflict. Each has advantages and disadvantages.
- Creating and sustaining a culture that is respectful and encourages employees to resolve conflicts effectively is important.
- Unproductive conflict occurs in organizations when employees do not share standards for guiding conduct and behavior, lack a common process for addressing conflict, and lack the skills for effective communication.
- Cooperative work is great for business.
- The conflict-mediation system encourages management and employees to resolve conflict at the lowest possible level.

CHAPTER 1 TOOLS AND ACTIVITIES

I. Conflict-Management Style Survey

Directions:

Listed below are ten questions, each with five possible responses, *A* through *E*. Place a *5* next to the response that you feel best describes you, *4* by the next best, and so on, with *1* being the least descriptive of you. There are no right and wrong answers. Enter a value for each response.

When you have strong feelings about a conflict situation you
_____ A. enjoy the emotional release and sense of accomplishment.
_____ B. enjoy the challenge of the conflict.
_____ C. are serious and concerned about how others are feeling and thinking.
_____ D. find it frightening because someone might get his or her feelings hurt.
_____ E. assume that there is nothing you can do to resolve the conflict.

What is the best result you can expect from a conflict?
_____ A. Conflict helps people face the facts.
_____ B. Conflict cancels out extremes in thinking so a middle ground can be reached.
_____ C. Conflict clears the air, enhances commitment, and ensures better results.
_____ D. Conflict demonstrates how silly it is to be self-centered and draws people together.
_____ E. Conflict assigns blame where it belongs.

If you are in charge of a situation that involves conflict, you
_____ A. make sure others know just how you see the issue.
_____ B. try to negotiate the best settlement.

_____ C. ask for other viewpoints and suggest that a position can be found that all sides might try.
_____ D. go along with others and provide support whenever you can.
_____ E. wait and see what everyone else has to say before taking a vote.

When someone else takes an unreasonable position on an issue, you
_____ A. lay it on the line and let them know you disagree.
_____ B. use humor or indirectly let them know you are not pleased.
_____ C. call attention to the conflict and explore mutually acceptable options.
_____ D. keep your misgivings to yourself.
_____ E. pretend not to care.

When you become angry with an employee or peer, you
_____ A. explode and let them know just how you feel.
_____ B. smooth things over with a good story or joke.
_____ C. express your anger and invite them to respond.
_____ D. act the opposite of your feelings.
_____ E. remove yourself from the situation and try to keep from having to interact.

When you find yourself disagreeing with others about something important, you
_____ A. stand by your convictions and argue strongly for them.
_____ B. appeal to the logic of the group and hope you can convince them you are right.
_____ C. explore points of view and search for alternatives that take everyone's views into account.
_____ D. go along with the group.
_____ E. don't get involved in the discussion, but also do not feel bound by any decision reached.

When one person takes a position opposite that of everyone else in the group, you
_____ A. point out that the individual is blocking group progress.
_____ B. make sure the individual has a chance to communicate his/her objection.
_____ C. try to uncover why the individual views the issue so that everyone understands.
_____ D. encourage group members to move on to an easier item on the agenda.
_____ E. remain silent and see what happens.

When you see a conflict emerging in your group, you
_____ A. push for a quick decision to ensure the task is completed.
_____ B. try to move the discussion to a middle ground where everyone feels comfortable.
_____ C. share your impression of what is going on so that the nature of the conflict can be discussed.
_____ D. defuse the situation with humor.
_____ E. stay out of the conflict as long as you can.

When faced with a conflict between two other group members, you
_____ A. tell them how they should resolve the situation.
_____ B. encourage them to identify possible areas of agreement.
_____ C. press for identification of shared concerns, goals, and actions.
_____ D. promote harmony because conflict will cause turmoil.
_____ E. wait and see how they address the issue.

In your view, what might be the reason for the failure of one group to work with another?
_____ A. Lack of a clearly stated position or failure to back up the group's position.

_____ B. Tendency of groups to force their leaders to abide by the group's decision as opposed to promoting flexibility, which would facilitate compromise.

_____ C. Tendency of groups to enter negotiations with a win-lose perspective.

_____ D. Lack of motivation on the part of the group's leaders, resulting in the leaders placing emphasis on maintaining their own power positions rather than addressing the issues involved.

_____ E. Irresponsible behavior on the part of the group's leaders, resulting in the leaders placing emphasis on maintaining their own power positions rather than addressing the issues involved.

Scoring:
Total all of the numbers you placed in each letter and record the results below. (For example, if you entered a 5 next to A on all ten questions, you would enter 50 next to A below.)

A: _____
B: _____
C: _____
D: _____
E: _____

Interpretation:
Look at your totals. The letter with the highest number represents the conflict-management style you feel most comfortable using. The lowest number represents the conflict-management style you probably use least.

Column A – Competitive Style
Column B – Compromising Style
Column C – Collaborative Style
Column D – Accommodating Style

Column E – Avoiding Style
Questions you may want to consider:
- What do your results suggest?
- Are you relying on one style to the detriment of others?
- Is reliance on your dominant style helpful to yourself and others?
- If not, what can you do to improve?

Assessing Your Organization's Level of Conflict

Take a few minutes to consider the following questions. You might complete this activity individually or with a group of individuals from your organization.

What are some examples of typical nonproductive conflicts encountered within your workplace between employees, administration, different departments, patients, and family members, etc.?

What do these unproductive conflicts cost employees, management, and the organization? Potential factors you might consider may include
- Grievances
- Turnover
- Production or services errors
- Litigation
- Poor communication
- Unnecessary meetings
- Lost sales
- Errors, mistakes, scrap, etc.
- Individual stress, sick leave, accidents on the job
- Sabotage
- Poor quality

If you could resolve conflict more effectively, how would it benefit employees, management, and employers? What observable difference would it make? (For example: If you think turnover would decrease, how much would it go down, and how would it affect employee morale, patient care, cost savings, etc.?)

Chapter 2
STANDARDS OF BEHAVIOR AND CONDUCT

*When you change the way you look at
things, the things you look at change.*
—Wayne Dyer

In This Chapter
The focus of this chapter is to examine the major components of the conflict-mediation system. You will learn that many organizations and individuals find it difficult to resolve conflict because they lack or fail to enact standards of conduct and behavior. As a result, people lack the trust needed to communicate effectively and address conflicts that occur. You will also learn the importance of shared values, dealing with power issues, following a method for resolving conflict, and creating an environment that is safe for dissent and personal growth. You will also read several cases that exemplify the importance of shared standards of conduct and behavior.

Today it is not uncommon to read of one healthcare system after another collapsing. Think about countries like Yemen or Venezuela. The war in Yemen has completely decimated the healthcare system. More than half of its citizens have little access to basic healthcare, less than 45 percent of the hospitals are operational, and the health personnel cannot cope with the needs. Even though Venezuela has the largest oil reserves in the world, it is struggling to stave off economic collapse as lower demand for oil and price controls lead to rocketing inflation. The impact on Venezuela's healthcare system has been heightened by exchange-rate controls, which has led to a shortage of the foreign currency needed to import equipment, food, and medicines. The Pharmaceutical Federation of Venezuela estimates the country is suffering from an 85 percent shortage of basic medicines amid an economic crisis also marked by severe hyperinflation and food scarcity. The entire Venezuelan healthcare system is on the verge of collapse, and the government knows it. Some hospitals lack electricity, and more than 13,000 doctors have left Venezuela in the past four years in search of better opportunities. Conflict in Yemen and Venezuela and in the healthcare organizations of these countries is rampant.

Fortunately, the United States and most countries are not like Yemen or Venezuela, but it is not uncommon to turn on the news or open a newspaper and learn of a company in court for inexcusable examples of corporate executive greed, financial malfeasance, and stock manipulation. For example, Mylan, Volkswagen, Wells Fargo, and other companies violated their own values and rules of conduct in a quest for greater profits. Even today, we see some pharmaceutical companies that have dramatically increased prices for vital medicines. We have also seen hospitals that have ignored claims of sexual harassment, bullying on the job, and discrimination. We have become accustomed to seeing executives award themselves huge pay increases, perks, and stock options while laying off earnest, dedicated employees. Employees and shareholders alike find themselves aghast at the lack of ethics, morality, and common decency exhibited by these executives and their boards of directors.

If ever there were a need for the leadership of healthcare organizations to truly live their values, and "walk the walk," now is the time. Individuals, families, communities, and healthcare organizations need standards that provide practical guidance for behavior and conduct. Values and ethical standards provide us with the rules and principles that allow us to build trust, work effectively with each other, and align our efforts for success. But *having* written organizational values, codes of conduct, and ethical standards and *living* them in act and deed every day are two different things.

The executives at many organizations—like Mylan, Enron, Volkswagen, and Wells Fargo—were masters of talking about the importance of fair, ethical standards and living up to their organizational values, but they also felt they were personally above these same standards and values in the pursuit of additional profits or personal gain. As you may recall, Mylan had to pay $465 million to resolve claims it overcharged the government for its EpiPen emergency allergy treatment, which became the center of a firestorm over price increases. The Enron Corporation depicts a company that reached dramatic heights only to collapse when regulators learned that it was deeply enmeshed in fake business holdings and off-the-books accounting. In 2015, Volkswagen admitted that many of its cars being sold in America had a "defeat device"—software in diesel engines that could detect when they were being tested, changing the performance accordingly to improve results. And Wells Fargo, under pressure to meet steep sales goals and incentives, encouraged employees to create over a million fraudulent accounts in their customers' names. These organizations are not unique; this happens far too often.

For ethical standards and values to be meaningful, they must be applied consistently to everyone within the organization and communicated clearly through both word and deed. When standards and values are given lip service, employees quickly understand that it is safe to ignore or disregard values and codes of conduct in pursuit of less honorable goals. Consider the following case example from the high-technology sector.

Recently, a high-technology manufacturer who made semiconductor components used in the computers and equipment of many healthcare instruments was struggling to maintain its market share in the very competitive industry segment. Stock analysts, industry experts, and its own internal employee-satisfaction surveys consistently suggested that this organization's employees and products were perceived as above average. However, the organizational culture was viewed as rigid, patriarchal, and overly competitive as evidenced by constant unproductive conflict, divisive rivalry between divisions within the company, high turnover rate among top performers, and an unwillingness of executives to look critically at their own internal behavior that resulted in several large sexual harassment or discrimination settlements.

In response to this criticism, the company decided that one solution to this dilemma was to develop a set of company values that would serve as standards for future conduct and behavior both internally and with its external customers. The company spent a considerable amount of money to hire a consulting firm to conduct meetings with representative groups of employees and managers at each domestic and international manufacturing or sales site that comprised its operations. From these meetings, a set of values were developed which were representative of all sites and country cultures. The public relations department worked closely with human resources to "roll out" the new values with great fanfare. Brochures were distributed, posters printed, and plans made to ensure all current and new employees were fully oriented to the new values.

At an all-manager meeting to introduce the values and share quarterly results, the chief executive officer opened with a few introductory remarks and then said, "Well, the HR department says

I need to talk about our values. Values are very important. We should respect others, remember that customer service is critical, and behave with integrity, honesty, and compassion." At this point, the CEO paused, smiled broadly, spread his arms wide and announced, "Now let's talk about what's *REALLY* important—making *MONEY!*"

It should not come as a big surprise that his audience understood his true message quite clearly: "The true standard of success in this organization is profits; how you get them is secondary. Let's get back to business as usual!" The executives and management of the company took his message to heart. Short-term financial results remained the order of the day. This mindset led to an intensification of the organization's existing culture of "look out for yourself," mistrust, and "cover-your-behind" thinking. As a result, in the following year, talented employees who were initially hopeful about a change in culture left, product design and production targets were missed, sales declined, profits fell, and its stock price plummeted.

As this case illustrates, as well as what occurred at Mylan, Volkswagen, and Wells Fargo, in an environment where duplicity, mistrust, and dishonesty prevail, it is extremely difficult to resolve conflicts constructively. One does not have to be the CEO of a Fortune 500 company to recognize that organizational survival in today's demanding and competitive environment is difficult. To collaborate effectively, organizations and individuals must manage conflict in ways that are conducive to building a synergistic and productive work environment. Inevitably, management and employees are going to have disputes over strategies, goals, roles, responsibilities, behavior, conduct, and resources. Nevertheless, like the players on professional sports teams, they must not only work through these disputes quickly, but in ways that achieve a positive solution AND build positive levels of trust and respect. In a world where patient care, product quality, and service delivery are vital, organizations that can productively manage day-to-day conflict will come out on top.

In this chapter, you will learn how organizations can work with employees to define standards for guiding behavior and conduct that help achieve a highly productive environment. As we saw in the previous chapter, in any sport there are standards which guide how the game is played, the physical dimensions of the playing area, tools or equipment with which the game is played, and rules that constitute proper and improper play. These standards provide structure, organization, and purpose for both the players and the fans. It is important to recognize that shared standards of behavior and conduct are not a constraint upon the game; rather, they allow the players to be as free and creative as possible within the framework of that sport. The same should be true for an organization. If everyone is playing by the same ethical standards of behavior, you create a fertile environmental for building trust, alignment, a climate of respect, cohesion, and synergy.

The conflict-mediation system recommended in this book is predicated upon positive standards for guiding behavior and conduct from which people may operate on a day-to-day basis. These standards provide all group members with a clear idea of what "success" looks like and define how the members will operate and support each other to achieve success. Success in your healthcare organization may be determined by quality of patient care, profitability, new products, better service, improved relationships, or any number of worthwhile outcomes. Success in your family may be personal growth, education, financial security, and healthy lifestyles.

Shared standards help guide your efforts and interactions with others, and allow you and others to know when you are "on track" or veering off course. When standards do not exist, or they exist but are ignored, we frequently see mistrust, misalignment, wasted effort, miscommunication, poor service, and employee turnover. The bottom line is that if healthcare organizations are unable to resolve conflict internally, they are going to be far less successful with their customers and other stakeholders.

We have found that standards for guiding behavior and conduct need to take into consideration at least four elements to develop a productive, motivating, and empowering workplace that achieves high-quality results:
1. Shared organizational values
2. The ability to manage and capitalize on differences in power
3. A method for facilitating the process of resolving conflict
4. A safe environment for dissent, growth, and development

We recognize there may be other elements that are particularly important in your industry or culture. Let's look at each of the four above in turn.

SHARED ORGANIZATIONAL VALUES

An organization's values answer the question, "What is important to us?" Values are the deep-seated, pervasive standards that influence every aspect of organizational life, including how decisions and judgments are made, how employees respond to others, if and how commitments are met, and how organizational goals are pursued. Employees are motivated and encouraged by values.

When values are clear, credible, and enacted consistently by everyone within an organization, employees do not have to look to someone in authority for direction. Rather, employees are able to act in a responsible fashion that benefits themselves and others over both the short and long-term. Further, when one works in an environment where work activities and values are united, individual and collective energy and motivation are aligned. Following are some examples of the values of several prominent healthcare organizations (Figure 3).

Cleveland Clinic	Pfizer	MD Anderson
Quality. We maintain the highest standards and achieve them by continually measuring and improving our outcomes. **Innovation.** We welcome change, encourage invention and continually seek better, more efficient ways to achieve our goals. **Teamwork.** We collaborate and share knowledge to benefit patients and fellow caregivers for the advancement of our mission. **Service.** We strive to exceed our patients' and/or fellow caregivers' expectations for comfort and convenience. **Integrity.** We adhere to high moral principles and professional standards by a commitment to honesty, confidentiality, trust,	**Customer Focus**: We are deeply committed to meeting the needs of our customers, and we constantly focus on customer satisfaction. **Community**: We play an active role in making every community in which we operate a better place to live and work, knowing that its ongoing vitality has a direct impact on the long-term health of our business. **Respect for People**: We recognize that people are the cornerstone of Pfizer's success. We value our diversity as a source of strength and are proud of Pfizer's history of treating employees with respect and dignity. **Performance**: We strive for continuous improvement in our performance, measuring	**Caring:** By our words and actions, we create a caring environment for everyone. We are sensitive to the concerns of our patients and our co-workers. We are respectful and courteous to each other at all times. We promote and reward teamwork and inclusiveness. **Integrity:** We work together to merit the trust of our colleagues and those we serve. We hold ourselves, and each other, accountable for practicing our values. We communicate frequently, honestly and openly. By our actions, we create an environment of trust. **Discovery:** We embrace creativity and seek new knowledge. We help each other to identify and solve problems. We seek personal growth and

Compassion. We demonstrate our commitment to world-class care by providing a caring and supportive environment for our patients, patients' families and fellow caregivers.	ensuring that integrity and respect for people are never compromised. **Collaboration**: We know that to be a successful company we must work together, transcending organizational and geographic boundaries to meet the changing needs of our customers. **Leadership**: We believe that leaders empower those around them by sharing knowledge and rewarding outstanding individual effort. We are dedicated to providing opportunities for leadership at all levels in our organization. **Integrity**: We demand of ourselves and others the highest ethical standards, and our products and processes will be of the highest quality. **Quality**: Quality is ingrained in the work of	We encourage learning, creativity and new ideas.

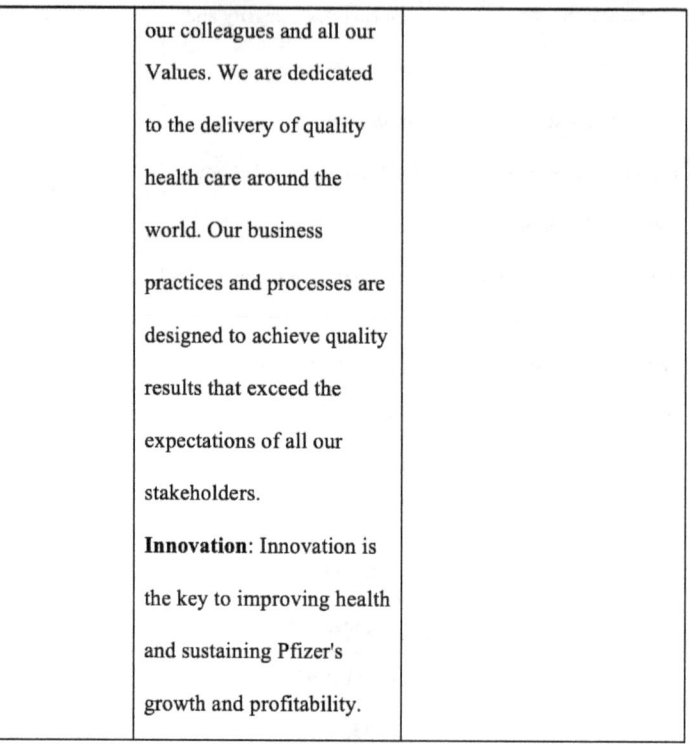

Figure 3: Organizational Values

If your healthcare organization has a set of values, they probably look similar to those listed above. In addition, if you look closely at your organization's values, and those of the Cleveland Clinic, Pfizer, and MD Anderson, you will probably notice some common themes. Some of the related values across these three organizations are respect for others, care and compassion, integrity, teamwork and collaboration, creativity, and quality. For any healthcare organization, these values make very good sense.

However, if employees do not feel the values of an organization are truly "lived," and that the organization does not really "walk the walk," you have an organizational culture in which unproductive conflict can run rampant. For example, imagine yourself working in an environment in which you do not feel respected or where you and others feel harassed, discriminated against, and bullied. Suppose you feel your thoughts, ideas, and input are not valued. Suppose you got into your profession because you truly believe caring for others is important, but you are routinely so overloaded, understaffed, and underappreciated that you feel constant stress and burnout? What if you have serious doubts about the integrity or intentions of upper management or coworkers? How are these feelings going to affect your integrity and focus on quality every day?

If this describes the environment in which you work, you are probably experiencing poor communication, too much turnover, grievances, and far too much unproductive conflict. Healthcare organizations that really want to be one of the "best places to work" and known for their high quality and skill are also those that pay close attention to ensuring that what they say in their values is reinforced and rewarded in the behavior of all employees—top to bottom.

The good news is that shared values can also provide a solid foundation for addressing conflicts that inevitably occur when the needs of the individual, group, and organization must be considered. Sometimes, the needs of the group and organization may outweigh the needs of the individual. On other occasions, the organization and group may decide to support the individual. For example, a group member may value both paying appropriate attention to their family and providing effective customer service. When faced with the need to stay late to respond to a customer service request, or leaving on time to honor a family responsibility, the employee can foster a constructive discussion with coworkers by communicating their values, their need, and find another solution so that both can be met.

POWER MANAGEMENT

Woodrow Wilson stated, "Power consists of one's capacity to link his will with the purpose of others, to lead by reason and a gift of cooperation." This is an important observation as power is an intangible force in any organization. Power may be defined as the potential for one person or department to influence other persons or departments. Power may also refer to the ability to achieve goals or outcomes that the power holder desires.

Textbooks typically recognize five sources of personal power. *Legitimate power* is the authority granted by the organization to the formal position a manager holds. For example, a manager has the legal authority to control and use organizational resources to accomplish the unit or department goals. *Reward power* is the ability to bestow rewards, promotions, raises, or even just a compliment or a "pat on the back" to others. As long as employees value the rewards, an organization can use reward power to influence behavior and action. *Coercive power* is the authority or ability to punish or recommend punishment to others. Punishments may involve demotion, suspension, job reassignment, or even withholding praise or other rewards. *Expert power* derives from a person's higher skill or knowledge about the tasks or job to be performed. Finally, *referent power* derives from the personal characteristics that people admire or identify with. Often, employees who are well liked and respected are also seen as the "go-to" people to help solve problems and lead teams. People with referent power are admired because of who they are, not just because of their expertise or ability to influence people, obtain resources, or achieve goals.

While these five forms of power are defined individually above, an individual can display several at once. For example, an individual might be an expert in their specialty, well liked by others, and serve as the office manager for a dentistry or veterinary practice. This individual is displaying expert, referent, and legitimate power all at once. And, as a manager, this individual also has the power to reward or punish an employee who reports to him or her.

Power management reflects the fact that employees at all levels bring capabilities that can help drive the organization or group forward. Power management is the process through which team members and employees recognize, appreciate, acknowledge, and work with these differences in legitimate authority, expert, reward, coercive, and referent power. In organizations where power is ineffectively applied, managers or employees may apply power in ways that instill fear, resentment, or hostility. For example, if a manager routinely makes decisions or judgments based upon his or her legitimate positional power and without any input from others, employees may cease to contribute, become argumentative, or avoid involvement altogether.

Effective organizations and effective managers recognize, as Woodrow Wilson observes above, that there is a role for each style of power. While one person may have legitimate authority to make a decision, in today's competitive, synergistic work environment, that individual should be open to sharing power with someone else that has exceptional expertise in an area. Organizations that manage power effectively ensure that all team members recognize, acknowledge, and maximize each other's skills, abilities, personalities, and relationships to ensure organizational success.

PROCESS LEADERSHIP

Effective groups and teams realize that it is often best to have someone serve as a group process facilitator. This person ensures that the group is true to its principles, focused on the issue being discussed, and that all members participate. While most group members may focus on the technical aspects of a problem, challenge, or opportunity, the group process facilitator focuses on how to help group members work and communicate effectively with each other.

Group process leaders should be skilled at helping others to evaluate problems, arrive at decisions, and develop action plans. Process facilitators use a variety of group methods such as brainstorming, force-field analysis, flowcharting, fish-bone and affinity diagrams, and multi-voting to ensure that all participants are heard and that all potential ideas or suggestions are shared.

Selecting a person or process facilitator does not impart any power to the person. In fact, this role can shift from member to member. The key is that the role of this individual is to focus on managing the conflict-mediation process, not the problem or challenge itself, by clarifying communication, recording thoughts, feelings, and suggestions, and assisting the group in the application of appropriate problem-solving and decision-making methods.

CREATING A SAFE ENVIRONMENT

Effective organizations create an environment where members feel it is safe to communicate with each other about opportunities, suggestions, ideas, and conflicts. A safe environment is one in which managers and employees feel recognized and appreciated for working well with others and enhancing group success. Abraham Maslow identified five levels of human motivation in his 1943 theory of human motivation based on a hierarchy of needs. This model is very useful for considering how a healthcare organization should structure itself and respond to employee needs in order to bring out the best in all employees. As presented in Figure 3, these five levels of human motivation are

- *physiological needs*, which include basic human biological functions such as hunger, thirst, sleep, and sex
- *safety and security needs*, or the requirement for a secure environment
- *love and social recognition*, or the need for belonging and connection others
- *esteem needs*, or the need to be regarded well in terms of achievement and recognition
- *self-actualization*, which is when people feel they are doing what they are best suited for, fulfilling life goals, and realizing their potential

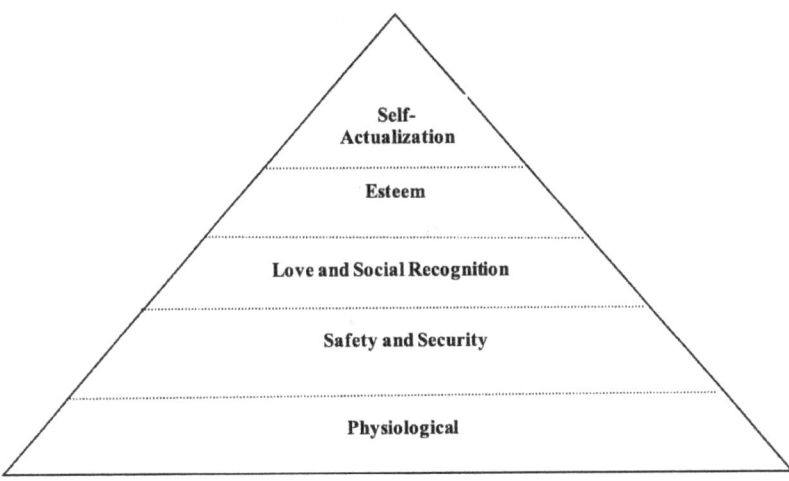

Figure 4: Maslow's Hierarchy of Needs

Most healthcare organizations are adept at meeting the basic physiological needs of their employees. As the hierarchy of needs suggests, a workforce that feels they are working in an environment that allows each employee to feel safe and secure is generally much more productive than one in which employees feel threatened. If an employee feels harassed, bullied, discriminated against, or that their job is always in jeopardy, he/she will not feel safe and secure.

A case in point occurred recently with a manufacturer of pharmaceuticals. One afternoon, one of the authors of this book was jogging with a colleague who had been working for this organization for the past twelve years. When asked how he was enjoying his work, he replied, "Morale and productivity are the pits! Last month, our executive vice president called the twenty individuals who comprise our research team into the conference room. Once we were assembled, he brought in eight guys from a country in the Far East and announced that our job was to train them over the next nine months to be able to do our jobs. At that point, eight of us would be fired. You can imagine how stunned our group was."

He shook his head as they jogged along and then continued, "You know what really stunk? These eight guys were as surprised as we were. No one had said anything to them other than they were here to be trained. They were embarrassed to have been put in that situation."

When asked how the employees were responding to this state of affairs, he said, "Well, in the following month our top four lead researchers left, along with two of the guys from the Far East team. Our work has ground to a near-standstill. We are not going to have our products tested and ready for sale in the original time frame. The company will miss out on millions in sales. And you know what really gets me? We will get blamed for the shortfall, and this shortsighted executive will get a bonus for cutting his manpower costs."

This example illustrates several key points. First, that the standards of behavior described in this chapter are all interconnected. The executive violated the company values which purport that "people are our greatest asset." This is clear from both the heartless manner in which he communicated this decision and his disregard for the feelings of both the home design team and the visiting employees from the Far East. Even though the employees had the communication skills to present their feelings, because the environment was not viewed as safe, no one bothered to confront him on his behavior or take the issue up with higher-level executives. Also, note that this announcement was made from a very strong position of legitimate authority; the executive made the decision with no input from those impacted. Finally, notice that he presented a completed solution. He did not meet with key individuals, lay out the conflict or the challenge or dilemma he was facing, and ask for their assistance in resolving the problem. Because of the shortsighted approach to resolving conflict, he created more problems than he solved.

A major prerequisite for a safe environment is for individuals, groups, management, and executives to be able to honestly and critically reflect on their own practices and behaviors. For example, at Mylan, Volkswagen, and Wells Fargo, despite their company values, it was not safe to point out the enormous gap between company standards for business conduct and actual practices. Effective healthcare organizations and leaders recognize that greater progress can be made when egos do not get in the way of values-driven improvement.

APPRECIATING DIVERSITY

The world is becoming increasingly diverse, and the need to work productively with people of different nationalities, religious upbringings, and variable language skills can have a positive and negative effect on conversations, productivity, and patient care. Therefore, it is wise not just to consider differences in personalities, but also to be aware that cross-cultural misunderstandings may increase the potential for unproductive conflict. Following are some potential causes or situations that can contribute to conflicts or misunderstandings:

- misunderstandings or conflict between different nationalities, or religious or ethnic groups
- cultural ignorance and insensitivity
- lack of awareness of different societal lifestyle practices
- differences in cultural practice
- differences in perception of illness and treatment
- miscommunication and misinterpretation.

When you work with people from culturally diverse backgrounds, often the difference in cultural values causes misunderstandings and possibly conflict that can hinder the development of trusting, supportive, and helpful relationships. There are six fundamental patterns of cultural differences, and these can all impact your healthcare organization's ability to address conflict with management, employees, customers, and patients.

Different verbal communication styles

Across cultures, some words and phrases are used in different ways. For example, "yes" can vary from "maybe I'll consider it" to "definitely yes." Depending on which version of yes you are looking for, the other person's response can affect what both of you view as consent to a course of action. When they say yes or tacitly agree to a worker's suggestion, it may not really mean that they do agree with the worker but rather that they do not want to offend the worker by disagreeing with them.

Different nonverbal communication styles

Nonverbal communication refers to facial expressions, gestures, seating arrangements, personal distance, and sense of time. For example, avoidance of eye contact is a sign of great respect in some cultures, whereas in other cultures, not looking at someone is considered very rude and may even suggest that the other person is not telling the truth.

Different attitudes toward conflict

Some cultures view conflict as a positive thing, while other cultures avoid conflict as much as possible. For example, many Eastern countries deal with their conflict quietly. In such cases, a written exchange might be the favored means to resolve the conflict.

Different approaches to completing tasks

People from different cultures tend to complete tasks differently. Some may be task-orientated, while others are relationship-orientated. For example, Asian cultures tend to attach more value to developing relationships at the beginning of a shared project and more emphasis on task completion toward the end. Conversely, Westerners tend to focus immediately on the task and let relationships develop as they work on that task. The fact that one group chooses task over relationship does not mean that they place different values on relationships or that they are less committed, rather that they just pursue different goals during the process.

Different decision-making styles

Decision-making roles vary widely from culture to culture. Some cultures delegate, while other cultures place higher value on holding decision-making responsibilities. When decisions are made in a group, some cultures may prefer majority rule, while others view consensus as the preferred mode for reaching a decision

Different attitudes toward disclosure

When you deal with a conflict, ensure that you are aware of how people may differ when it comes to expressing emotions. Some questions that need to be asked—such as "What was the conflict about?"—may seem intrusive and personal to some people. Taking time to build rapport and demonstrate empathy can significantly enhance the quality of communication.

The best way to work with people from different cultures is to be aware that cultural diversity exists and to talk about the differences. You need to remember that it can be difficult to address cultural differences without resorting to stereotypes. Stereotypes should not exist, as no person is exactly like another person, and no individual is a clone of another member in the same group. Also, as the level of diversity in an organization grows, so does the complexity of communication and the necessity to make greater effort in improving communication skills. The good news is that while diversity can introduce some challenges, diversity also creates opportunities for character development by teaching tolerance and respect and encouraging concern for equity for people from culturally diverse backgrounds.

THE SYNERGY of STANDARDS

We have found that these four elements—shared organizational values, the ability to manage and capitalize on differences in power, a method for facilitating the process of resolving conflict, and a safe environment for dissent, growth, and development—collectively provide a framework for establishing standards for guiding both behavior and conduct. However, legitimate attention must be paid to evaluating organizational standards and making improvements as needed. Nothing demotivates employees faster than executives who purport to live according to a high standard of conduct but in fact act in violation of those standards.

Ken Lay, the CEO of Enron, spoke frequently and eloquently on the need for honesty, high ethical standards, and integrity. As we now know, Enron's actual practices in these areas were highly unethical. At the high-technology firm discussed earlier in this chapter, the senior vice president in charge of human resources was nicknamed "Slick" by other company executives. He was given this nickname in recognition of his ability to help executives avoid lawsuits following questionable business practices or employee relationships. His vice president of human resources, a married man whose wife also worked for him, was having an affair with the manager of compensation, one of his direct reports. When the affair was discovered by his wife, he was allowed to continue to manage both women for a six-month period, after which his wife left the company and filed for divorce.

If this was the behavior that existed in the human resources department, which was directly tasked with overseeing the implementation of company values, one can imagine what type of behavior was taking place in other departments! Not surprisingly, employees viewed company values, codes of conduct, and standards of behavior as superficial maxims that had little to no real meaning.

On the other hand, there are also organizations which are widely regarded for their ability to speak openly and honestly, who are able to resolve conflict effectively, and who adhere tenaciously to their standards of conduct and behavior. Companies such as Southwest Airlines, the Container Store, Zappos, Whole Foods, and Starbucks are widely regarded for establishing cultures which are open, honest, highly synergistic, and ultimately, very profitable.

For example, Herb Greenberg, analyst for CBS Marketwatch,

observes that Howard Schultz, former CEO of Starbucks, is consistently perceived as one of the best CEOs in the country. Greenberg notes, "I believe the tone of a company filters down from the top. Schultz created the vision, instilled a culture that gave more than lip service to employee values, and allowed his company to continue to put up with critics like me. Unlike CEOs who challenge the naysayers, and even attack them, Schultz appeared to begrudgingly respect them. And while he's highly cognizant of his company's stock price, rather than running his business for Wall Street, he runs it for his customers and employees. To Schultz, in the end, it's all about the coffee." Both employees and customers appear to agree, given the stellar customer service, high-quality product, and continuing company growth.

Kouzes and Posner address the need for high standards in their book, *Credibility*, observing that

> people still want and need leadership. They just want leaders who hold to an ethic of service and are genuinely respectful of the intelligence and contributions of their constituents. They want leaders who will put principles ahead of politics and other people before self-interests. (2003, xvii)

To a leader that has the conviction of his beliefs, words like *value* and *respect* must be backed up with hard decisions and actions. The *real* test of leadership is maintaining those convictions during change and upheaval.

Let's consider another case example to understand how an organization can choose to recognize an improvement opportunity and adhere to its values and principles.

Carestone is an assisted living center in a small town in south Texas. Assisted living provides senior citizens a place to stay where they are provided all the comforts of home, plus they have access to medical services. Last year, a family member of one of the residents of Carestone went to the administrator to ask if their mother could be given her daily medications in her room. Typically, medications were given to her at mealtime in the dining room, and the mother did not like having to take so many medications in front of other residents. The administrator immediately saw a problem, *conflict*. If the mother was allowed to have medicines in her room rather than the dining room, the other residents would want access to that same privilege. What was the administrator to do?

In this case, both the administrator and the family member talked about the need to have medications in the dining room versus the living quarters. From the administrator's perspective, there were not enough staff to ensure each resident got the appropriate medications in their room; after all, the delivery of medications had to be by a nurse. The family member did not know that the medications had to be delivered by a nurse and could understand the administrator's view. The problem was one of convincing the mother that her issue of taking meds in front of others was understood but needed to be overcome.

Following is another example of a senior executive who was able to respond in a positive way to a situation that was well intended but was not implemented as he had expected. While this example is not in the healthcare industry, the dynamic involving a good idea, work teams, professional egos, and lack of effective communication can happen in any organization.

DrugCom was a manufacturer of pharmaceutical products for the healthcare industry. In this very competitive business, the executives were always seeking new methods for improving their products and profitability. DrugCom's vice president of production noticed that competitors and other related companies were achieving significant improvements through the use of work teams in the production. Articles he read and discussions with experts in the field suggested that both employee morale and operational production could be improved dramatically with these teams. A key feature that caught his attention among his study of other successful efforts was the need to improve the technical, analytic, and team-building skills and knowledge of the production-equipment technicians. At the vice president's direction, the training department contracted with an external vendor to provide team-building workshops, and another vendor to offer courses in statistical process control and quality-improvement techniques.

The technicians were delighted with the new workshops. DrugCom's equipment technicians were a hardworking, dedicated group who spent a great deal of time monitoring the equipment. In the course of their training, the technicians were informed that they were to apply their new skills and knowledge to improving product quality, reducing scrap, and increasing production. However, after completing their training, when the technicians made recommendations to the engineering staff and their management, their suggestions were minimized or just ignored. The technicians felt they spent significantly more time around the equipment than the engineers and resented that their advice was not appreciated—particularly when they were told in their training program that they were to give advice in the first place.

It quickly became apparent that neither the technician's management nor the engineering staff was very supportive of the effort. First, managers and engineers felt that when mistakes happened, they would be the ones held accountable. Second, they felt that only individuals with a college degree in an engineering field had the skills needed to diagnose improvement needs and understand how a small change in one area affects the manufacturing process downstream. Both management and engineers also observed that the technicians did not know how to provide the data engineers needed to make good decisions and take action. Rather, the technicians simply suggested changes based on what appeared to be "gut feelings" or simple observations. As a result, when the technicians suggested a change, the engineers felt it was easiest to ignore it.

After a few months, conflicts between management, the engineering staff, and the manufacturing technicians reached a critical point. Despite the cost of training the technicians, the vice president of production was seeing little, if any, improvement. In fact, it was clear that morale was going down, not up. The relationship between the technicians and engineers was not improving, and the technicians were becoming increasingly vocal about this effort being "just another useless program of the month." In fact, two technicians quit during this period to take a job with a competitor. This caused additional delays since fewer staff was available to respond to maintenance issues, and the department incurred increased costs to recruit, hire, and train two new replacements. To address this problem, a meeting was held to discuss the conflict with the vice president of production, representatives from the engineer and technician job specialties, and a conflict-management facilitator.

During the meeting, several issues became evident. First, it became clear that the need for this effort and the vice president's rationale had not been well communicated to the first-line managers or engineering staff. Second, the first-line managers and engineering staff were very unclear regarding how this effort would affect their job security. To them, the idea of teams made sense on one level, but their role as a part of or supporter to the team was not explained. Understandably, management and the engineers were also concerned that they were the ones who would be held accountable for keeping the equipment operating. Their perspective was summed up by one manager who noted, "Sure, it's great for the technicians to give their input, but it is my job that is in jeopardy if something goes wrong!" An additional problem was that neither the first-line managers nor engineers understood *what* training the technicians were receiving, and consequently did not trust their skill level. Further, their highly technical training required that recommendations be founded on cold, hard facts—not suggestions that were not backed up with data.

Fortunately, the VP of production viewed conflict as a natural part of life, an opportunity to improve, and acted quickly in alignment with the company standards for guiding conduct and behavior. Modeling company values, the VP stressed that he appreciated this information, valued the thoughts of all present, acknowledged that he had made a mistake in not communicating the effort effectively or appropriately involving management, engineers, and technicians in the design and implementation of the effort. He also stressed the need to remain true to company values for profitability, quality, and customer service.

In response, the VP of production tasked a new workgroup comprised of representatives from management, engineering, and technicians with redesigning the work-team initiative. This group ensured that both first-line management and engineers were involved in understanding the training currently being provided to technicians and identifying additional skills needed. Further, instead of having outside vendors present the technical content, several engineers volunteered to teach these workshops. It was also clear that while the technicians had received team training, the engineers and managers had not. To correct this mistake, managers and engineers attended training which clarified their role on work teams and provided skills in team leadership. The technicians were thrilled to be learning more advanced skills and excited at the opportunity to work with the engineers on quality-improvement projects. Finally, the engineers volunteer to serve as on-the-job mentors to the technicians. This latter effort helped the engineers and technicians to get to know each other better, become confident of each other's skills, and ensured that the technicians were receiving the best training in areas the engineers felt were vital to production improvement.

This case illustrates how an individual (the VP of production) and an organization can choose to respond to a conflict in a manner that drives improvement. Rather than defend his ego as the executives for Bright Futures did in chapter one, this VP admitted his error and then acted decisively to encourage positive change. Company values were reinforced. All affected job specialties were trained in team-building techniques that included power-management skills in collaborative data collection, decision-making, problem-solving, communication, and meeting management. Process leadership was strengthened and encouraged when it became routine for meetings and conflicts to be facilitated by skilled process facilitators drawn from all three job levels. Finally, the safety of the work environment was reinforced by making it clear that it was okay to make and correct mistakes, that all jobs were secure, and that the thoughts, observations, and suggestions for improving productivity and work life from any employee were valued.

Because of this redefined team-building effort, scrap was significantly reduced, quality increased, costs declined, and revenues increased. The vice president of production also found that morale and teamwork improved dramatically, resulting in a lower turnover rate across all job specialties. Consequently, the company had to spend far fewer dollars on recruiting, interviewing, hiring, relocating, and training new employees. Sixteen months later, the vice president of production indicated, "There is no doubt that the investment in time and money we made to launch this process has paid off very well. Production and quality are up, morale is great, and we have individuals of all job grades working well together in teams. Admittedly we had to take a step backwards, but now we are really moving forward!"

VIOLATING STANDARDS

It would be very hard to be oblivious to the growing tidal wave of awareness of bullying and harassment in the workplace. Across the country, there is a rising emphasis in healthcare on ensuring that daily tasks and practices keep patients safe from harm, medical errors, and preventable adverse events. While it is important to consider safety efforts such as reducing the risk of falls, infections, and medication dosing errors, patient safety is also influenced by the way healthcare professionals interact with each other. This is precisely why it is critical that healthcare organizations provide all employees with appropriate conflict-management skills and an organizational culture where it is easy to surface and address conflict quickly and productively.

As noted in earlier chapters, unproductive conflict between employees in the workplace can undermine professional collaboration, quality, communication, and trust, which in turn may place patients at risk. Unproductive conflict between employees may include

- bullying and/or hostility between peers
- bullying and/or hostility by one person who has authority over another person
- verbal abuse, outbursts, and yelling
- passive aggressive acts such as ignoring messages, refusing to answer questions, etc.
- unprofessional behavior to others, including an impatient or condescending attitude, eye-rolling, throwing things, sarcasm, etc.
- violence (physical violence, throwing things, damaging equipment, or more dangerous behavior)

As these examples illustrate, any class of healthcare professional can be involved in these acts, including pharmacists, nurses, administrators, physicians, lab technicians, and others employees or patients. When positive relationships break down between healthcare providers, patient safety is directly threatened. For example, one survey found high numbers of healthcare providers who reported they had personally avoided interacting with another employee or manager to the point of not clarifying vague orders or feeling pressured to dispense a medication despite concerns about its safety. While this sounds outrageous, in real life if you know someone is going to yell at or belittle you for asking a question or voicing a concern, you are far less likely to seek that person out for a conversation or confront them with concerns. This holds true whether the bullying, harassing, or intimidating person is another nurse, a physician, or an administrator.

That cultures could exist in healthcare organizations where toxic behaviors are allowed is hard to fathom. A physician's assistant we spoke with who works at the Mayo Clinic observed, "In a profession whose purpose is about caring for others, we do a horrible job of caring for ourselves and each other!" Christine Nielsen, CEO of CJMLS, agreed and noted, "There is one unavoidable truth about life in the lab which we often gloss over: the cultures of healthcare organizations can be terrible. Toxic, even. There is something about the healthcare environment that seems to breed conflict. Yet these very places are supposed to be spaces of healing."

When constant unproductive conflict, bullying, and disruptive behaviors are not addressed, your healthcare professionals may also choose to leave the workplace or even leave the profession entirely. Having fewer staff than you need to provide care or an employee who is so stressed that they spend each day fearful of coming to work, or who is contemplating leaving, can also have a negative impact on quality, patient care, and patient safety. Since bullying and harassment are the two biggest challenges healthcare organizations face in terms of unproductive conflict on the job, these two issues will be covered below in more detail.

Bullying

Bullying in the workplace can take the form of verbal abuse; threatening, intimidating, or humiliating behaviors; and interference with another person's ability to complete work—all of which can affect patient safety, morale, and efficiency. Bullying can occur when the person who is the bully and the victim are on the same level, as in situations where one employee bullies another employee. However, bullying can also occur when managers or senior professionals intentionally intimidate subordinates or less skilled professionals.

Bullying can also occur when patients, family members, customers, or suppliers bully healthcare professionals. In any form, bullying in the workplace creates a toxic environment that affects not only the individual being bullied, but also observers and, potentially, patients or customers.

In a recent study, 4,884 healthcare workers, including nurses, pharmacists, physicians, and quality-management staff, were surveyed about workplace violence and harassment. Seventy-seven percent reported that they had encountered other clinical staff that communicated in a hostile manner, including a "reluctance or refusal to answer questions or return calls." In addition, 68 percent reported that they had experienced "condescending language or demeaning comments," and 18 percent of respondents reported they had objects thrown at them by another employee or manager.

Conflict that occurs from bullying can have major repercussions for any healthcare organization. For example, in one large healthcare facility, up to 70 percent of nurses left their jobs after being bullied, and according to *American Nurse Today*, roughly 60 percent of new RNs quit their first job within six months of being bullied (Townsend 2011). Not surprisingly, research in the *Journal of Nursing Management* has also found a strong correlation between conflict from bullying and the turnover rate of healthcare staff.

Clearly, negative conflict from bullying impacts patients, employees, and customers. A 2017 study published in the *International Emergency Nursing Journal* observes that when managers or employees simply stand by during incidents of bullying, the result is a culture in which maintaining the status quo and fear of retaliation can lead to *more* bullying and a decline in patient care. Patrick Beaver, chief nursing officer at East Cooper Medical Center in Mount Pleasant, South Carolina, put a fine point on this by noting, "There's a direct link between bullying and poor patient outcomes. Staff get distracted by a strong personality or derailed by a bully, and it takes their focus away from providing quality care."

To improve the workplace culture, healthcare organizations need to establish an environment where all employees can work through difficult circumstances, and where procedures are put in place to prevent this type of bullying from recurring. In addition, all employees must have the skills to address conflict and be encouraged to be vigilant and to take action to do what is necessary to identify bullies and ensure a safe, productive workplace.

Harassment

Healthcare organizations have known for a long time that ignoring harassment may also expose them to significant legal liability from unproductive conflict that impacts employees and potentially patient or customer care. Whether you have experienced it firsthand or have witnessed it, harassment is on the rise. Studies have shown that nearly half of American workers have been affected by workplace harassment in one form or another.

There are a number of factors that make a healthcare organization prone to experiencing harassment that leads to unproductive conflict. These factors include the traditional hierarchical organizational structure, a male-dominated environment, and frequently, a culture that allows or ignores instances of harassment—particularly when committed by those with power. The prevalence of harassment can be understood when one considers that 30 to 70 percent of female physicians and as many as half of female medical students report being sexually harassed. And this is in institutions where "do no harm" is the watchword!

With all of the scrutiny provided by recent high-profile cases involving harassment in corporations, the entertainment industry, and healthcare across the country, there seems to be more and more examples of organizations that have been successfully sued and received intense media attention. For example,

A federal appeals court ruled that a hospital in New England could be held responsible for an employee's sexual harassment of a coworker. Even though the hospital had a policy prohibiting sexual harassment and an internal reporting system to investigate claims, a three-judge panel unanimously upheld a jury verdict that the hospital should have known about its employee's misbehavior and taken appropriate actions to prevent it. As a result of the ruling, the harassed employee received an award of $125,000.

A federal jury in California awarded an employee $168 million, potentially the largest judgment in US history for a single victim of workplace sexual harassment. The award capped a trial in which the former physician assistant at Mercy General Hospital in Sacramento alleged she filed multiple complaints to no avail during her two-year tenure.

As with bullying, harassment at work can have serious consequences for the harassed individual as well as for other employees who experience it secondhand. The consequences to the individual employee can be many and serious. In some situations, a harassed employee may fear losing his or her job or the chance for a promotion if he or she refuses to give in to the sexual demands of someone in authority. In other situations, the unwelcome sexual conduct of coworkers or management makes the working conditions hostile and unpleasant, putting indirect pressure on the employee to leave the job entirely. And sometimes, the employee is so distressed by the harassment that they suffer serious emotional and physical consequences and may become unable to perform their job properly. According to data compiled by Equal Rights Advocates, 90 to 95 percent of sexually harassed workers suffer from some debilitating stress, including anxiety, depression, headaches, sleep disorders, weight loss or gain, nausea, lowered self-esteem, and sexual dysfunction. In addition, victims of sexual harassment lose $4.4 million dollars in wages and 973,000 hours in unpaid leave each year in the United States.

The bottom line is that unproductive conflict in the form of incivility, bullying, or harassment is something that your healthcare organization simply cannot tolerate. Even if we ignore the huge financial cost of losing a lawsuit to an employee who has been bullied or harassed, hiring and training new staff to replace those who leave is very costly. A literature review in the *Journal of Nursing Management* estimates that the cost of replacing a nurse is $27,000 to $103,000. And research by the Society of Human Resource Management indicates it can take approximately forty-two days to fill a vacant position. In addition, the healthcare organization will lose valuable institutional knowledge when a talented staff member leaves due to bullying or dissatisfaction with the workplace environment.

One final note is that bullying, incivility, harassment, and unproductive conflict are often viewed as simply something one person needs to work through with another person. In fact, the effect of these negative behaviors goes far beyond the person who is bullied or harassed, and the person who is doing the bullying or harassing. The effect on the morale of all employees can also be serious. Both men and women in a workplace can find their work disrupted by harassment even if they are not directly involved. Sexual harassment in particular can have a demoralizing effect on everyone within range of it, and it often negatively affects company productivity and patient safety. Non-victims, which can be other employees, suppliers, customers, or patients, frequently serve as bystanders or observers of this behavior.

Research is clear that even these non-victims experience stress and concern, often because they are wondering if they will be targeted next. Further, their level of trust that they are safe and that management or human resources will respond appropriately is diminished. One individual we spoke with concurred with this sentiment, noting, "I see harassment and bullying going on all the time and I keep worrying I am next. Why won't management stop this? Everyone sees what is going on, and management keeps sweeping it under the rug as if it never happens!"

Patients and customers also notice the presence of unproductive conflict. Recall the example shared in chapter one in which the parents of twin newborns observed constant unproductive conflict during their six-day stay in the hospital. How many of their friends do you think they have shared this story with?

So, what does this all mean for healthcare organizations? It means you should create a working environment that neither accepts nor engages in any type of behavior that breaks down professional communication and collaboration. If you have managers, physicians, nurses, or other employees that are inclined to snap at others who have questions, observations, or simply need more direction, these individuals may be undermining a culture of safety. If employees avoid reporting workplace bullying, intimidation, or harassment, perhaps from a fear of retaliation, the organization has a culture in which trust is low. Collaboration is key—and to ensure clear communication and cooperation, all employees, and particularly executives and managers, need to demonstrate greater leadership abilities, create a culture of trust, and train all employees to recognize and report unproductive conflict when they see it.

Even the most committed, motivated, well-meaning individual occasionally makes a mistake or takes an action that is in opposition to group standards or steps on someone else's toes. It is important to recognize that our negative reactions to others are often unintentional and not always directed at anyone in particular. A stressful morning getting the kids off to school, a lingering cold, a traffic jam, spilled coffee on one's desk, or any number of other minor irritants can cause us to behave or react to others in ways that we would agree are not productive.

Team members can continue to build trust and maintain group integrity by defining standards for guiding behavior and conduct, and developing the skills to address the transgression in a way that is supportive and understanding. When a supportive coworker helps us become aware that we have violated a shared value or communicated in a way that was hurtful, it is easier for us to make improvements and behave in a way that we have already agreed is best for everyone. When situations of conflict allow for an unsafe, unfair, or unethical environment, team members are more likely to respond with avoidance, accommodation, or competitive methods.

In this chapter you have learned that collaborative decision-making can result only if the organization and employees are committed to standards of conduct and behavior, and are skilled in the use of a mediation process that encourages the search for understanding and growth. Organizations which have developed but do not live in accordance to their values tend to encounter higher levels of unproductive conflict. Having a shared process for encouraging positive discussion allows all parties to maintain face, and feel they are "heard" and valued. This process will be examined in the next chapter.

The Least You Need to Remember

- Standards provide us with a sense of rules or principles for building trust, encouraging us to work productively with each other and align our efforts for success.
- Values must be lived to be believed.
- Power management means all employees are allowed to utilize their capabilities to help encourage productive growth.
- A process leader helps keep the group true to its principles and the issues being discussed, and ensures everyone is heard.
- Effective organizations strive to create an environment where members feel safe to communicate openly and honestly with each other.
- When standards are consistently violated, employees will begin to respond with avoidance, accommodation, or competitive methods.

CHAPTER 2 TOOLS and ACTIVITIES

Assessing Standards of Conduct and Behavior

Take a few minutes to reflect upon and answer the following questions individually or with a group of colleagues.

1. Does my organization have values or other standards that guide conduct and behavior between management, employees, and customers?
2. Are these values and standards fully understood and shared by all managers and employees?
3. Are our organizational values and standards *applied* fairly and consistently across all stakeholders?
4. Do all employees feel safe and encouraged to share their skills and talents and to speak openly and respectfully to others regardless of position? If not, why not?
5. Do we have skilled process facilitators to help us problem-solve, make decisions, and address conflict?
6. Is our work environment one in which employees are safe to communicate with each other about opportunities, ideas, and conflicts?

Chapter 3
THE CONFLICT-CONCERNS-GOALS-ACTIONS PROCESS

*Nothing is as powerful
as an idea whose time has come.*
—Victor Hugo

In This Chapter

While it would be nice if conflict were a rare occurrence, in reality it is a major factor of our personal and organizational lives. In this chapter we examine the second element of the conflict-mediation system. The conflict-mediation process is a means for introducing rationality into what can be a fairly emotional practice—that of addressing conflicts. You will learn that the conflict-mediation process is composed of four steps: identifying the conflict; understanding needs, concerns and motives; clarifying goals; and developing a plan of action. You will have a number of opportunities to examine how others have applied this process in order to resolve conflict.

Conflict has been with us from the dawn of time. Imagine, for a moment, the first time a caveman built a fire. Once the fire was roaring, it is not too hard to picture the following reactions from his fellow cave-dwellers:

"This is really great. I feel warm for the first time since the Ice Age!!"

"Hey, who built a fire where I usually sleep?"

"The fire is making too much smoke! Put it out."

"The fire is too small. Put more wood on it."

"Well, I think it's nice, but don't expect me to go get any firewood; it's not part of *my* job."

"First it was clubs, then wearing hides, now we have fire. When is all this change going to end?"

As this example suggests, conflict was a fact of life eons ago and remains a fact of life today. In healthcare organizations, educational institutions, government agencies, and companies across the country, what one person sees as an opportunity, another sees as an imposition. What one views as a waste of time and energy, another might view as a critical requirement for achieving an important goal. Conflict naturally exists when people are in disagreement or opposition.

There are three reasons why we seem to experience unproductive conflict. First, people think that their perspective of the world is shared by everyone else. As a result, we frequently do not take time to consider or understand the perspective that others bring. The following joke illustrates this point.

A middle-aged woman was visiting a new physician for a routine checkup. As she waited for the doctor to enter, she glanced around the waiting room and noticed his diploma from medical school on the wall. She was surprised to see that the name on the diploma was the same as a boy she had known in high school. However, when the portly, balding physician entered the room, the woman thought, "No, this can't be him."

However, as the physician began to ask questions about her medical history, she noticed that his voice and mannerisms were familiar. Finally, she could not contain herself and asked, "Excuse me, but you did go to Smithfield High School?"

"Why yes," he replied. "Why do you ask?"

"Oh, how wonderful," she exclaimed excitedly. "I had you in my class!"

The physician looked at her quizzically for a few moments and then said, "Really? What did you teach?"

As you probably surmise, in this story both the woman and the physician see each other very differently. In our experience this mirrors how different people view the world and the conflicts they have with others. We see life through our eyes, and not the eyes of others.

The second reason we experience so much conflict is that we each have expectations we assume that others also share. For example, at work, you have expectations regarding your role and responsibilities to the organization, how you will interact with management and coworkers, and what the organization needs to provide to you in terms of pay, safety, benefits, resources, recognition and appreciation, and job support. As long as the organization, management, and coworkers meet our expectations, and we meet the expectations of the organization, management, and coworkers, everything is fine. But when expectations are not met, conflict occurs.

Third, conflict is an inevitable element of interpersonal, organizational, family, and community life. Because conflict is often accompanied by strong emotions, people have a tendency to view conflict as negative and disruptive. As we learned in chapter one, this is not necessarily the case. When conflict is not resolved constructively, negative consequences result. When conflict prevents the attainment of interpersonal, organizational, family, or community objectives, it is viewed as dysfunctional conflict. However, conflict can also be very positive. When variations in beliefs, strategies, goals, or needs lead to the achievement of interpersonal, organizational, family, or community objectives, it is a result of functional or cooperative conflict.

Recall that the conflict-mediation system is comprised of three critical elements:

- Principles for guiding behavior and conduct
- A process for resolving conflicts
- Effective communication skills

In the previous chapter, you learned how important it is to develop principles for guiding daily behavior and interaction. These principles are very important for establishing an environment in which values are shared, communication skills are enacted, power differences are managed, and a safe environment for dissent, growth, and development is ensured.

This chapter presents a process for assisting individuals to work collaboratively with others to clarify, discuss, and reason through difficult issues in such a manner that negative emotions are kept to a minimum. This process encourages managers and employees to think through conflicts in a logical, transparent fashion so that the surface conflict is agreed to by all involved, underlying needs and motivations are clarified, goals are explored, and an action plan is developed that is agreed to and supported by all involved.

CONFLICT-MEDIATION PROCESS

In today's busy work environment, employees generally advance in their profession because they are good problem solvers. How you go about solving problems and dealing with conflict may vary depending on your job, the people you work with, and the situation. For example, you may solve problems by responding to patient needs, improving protocols, or improving software to enhance organizational success and efficiency. This may involve working closely with coworkers, management, vendors, suppliers, family members, and customers. While your problem-solving ability is an asset on one hand, it can also be a liability. Because of the speed at which business appears to change, external pressures from upper management or team members, and your own internal needs, you probably have a tendency to jump directly from identifying a problem to applying a solution—often with good intentions that are not clear to others. Consider the following example.

Randy, a pharmacy technician in the Apex Drug Store, is in the stockroom sorting the latest shipment of drugs when Tara, a new employee, walks up.

"Randy, I have a customer out front who wants to buy a package of twenty-four-hour allergy medicine that we normally keep behind the counter. I have looked around and I can't find this item. Do you know where this product is?"

Randy sets down the box of medical supplies he has in his hand and says, "No problem, I'll take care of this."

He walks to the counter and explains to the lady that the store is out of the twenty-four-hour allergy medicine but that a new shipment is expected the very next day. He goes on to say he will be glad to call her when the item is in so she can come pick the medicine up.

The woman agrees and he writes down her name and phone number. When the woman leaves, he turns around to see Tara is seething.

"What's the matter?" he asks.

"Why did you do that?" Tara asks sharply. "The only thing I wanted you to do is tell me what I should tell the lady. I like to work with my own customers."

Randy stutters, "Wait, I was just trying to help."

"Yeah, sure," Tara retorts. "What you did was make me look like an idiot in front of that lady!"

What went wrong?

As you can tell from the dialogue above, when this incident occurred, Randy was surprised by Tara's reaction. In his mind, he thought he was being helpful to Tara by demonstrating how to handle this customer's request. Tara clearly saw this in a different light. Now Apex Drug Store has a potential conflict on its hands. While this might appear to be a relatively minor matter, we have all seen "minor conflicts" escalate to crisis conditions. If this conflict is not cleared up, tension may build up between these two employees, and they may try to gather allies among other workers and speak poorly of each other to the manager. Ultimately, customers could notice the tension, sales may drop, and Randy or Tara could leave the store.

These types of conflicts occur all the time at work, at home, and in our communities. However, keep in mind that conflict does not have to be negative. If responded to in a thoughtful, respectful manner, just about any conflict can be turned into an opportunity to build trust, accountability, and growth. On the other hand, as you have probably experienced firsthand, if the people involved respond defensively, disrespectfully, and with the wrong tone, the conflict and negative outcomes simply worsen.

We have found that a very effective method for addressing conflicts is to follow a simple four-step process that we call the *Conflict-Mediation Process* (Figure 5). We will also refer to this as the CCGA process—for **C**onflict, **C**oncerns, **G**oals, and **A**ctions.

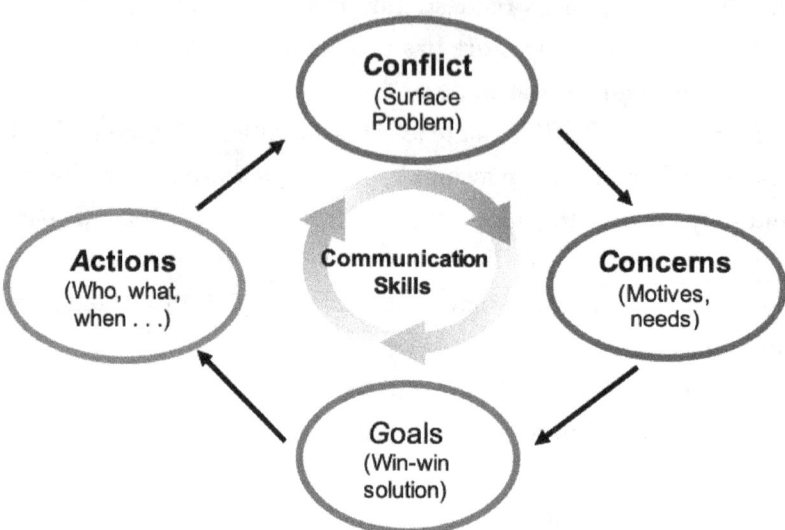

Figure 5: Conflict-Mediation Process

Step One: Identify the Conflict

The first step in the conflict-mediation process is for those involved to come to an agreement regarding the nature of the conflict. Keep in mind that those affected by a conflict might include not only the individuals or groups most intimately involved in the conflict, but also other key stakeholders who may or may not be present, and the organization itself.

In the example above, the people affected by this conflict certainly include Randy and Tara. Potentially other employees, the store management, and customers could be affected. Let's assume that in the example above, when Tara expressed her displeasure to Randy, there were no other customers waiting and he could respond to her immediately. (If other customers *were* present, he could respond as soon as convenient.) Let us also assume that Randy has attended training in the conflict-mediation process and in effective communication skills. In keeping with the first step of the conflict-mediation process, Randy begins his reply by tactfully and respectfully describing what he views as the conflict, and gives Tara a chance to respond and offer her view.

"Tara," Randy says, "I want to apologize for this misunderstanding. I should not have taken your request for help to mean I should wait on the customer. Is that how you see it?"

Tara replies, "Well yeah, I did not expect you to wait on the customer. I just wanted to know what I should do."

Step 2: Clarify Concerns

The conflict which both Tara and Randy have agreed upon is that Randy waited on the customer when Tara just wanted to be told what to do. Now, as an effective problem solver, the easiest thing for Randy to do is to jump straight to a solution and say he will try to remember to explain procedures to Tara in the future and not wait on her customers. However, he does not know *why* she reacted so angrily, and jumping directly to a solution may just address the tip of the iceberg. An iceberg, as you know, is a huge piece of ice. The reason an iceberg is dangerous is that roughly 90 percent of its mass is underwater. While we can see what is above the water, it is what is below the surface that sinks ships (remember the *Titanic*).

The same is true with any conflict. Everyone has their view of what the problem or opportunity (conflict) is, and they also have, in their mind, a very good reason for feeling that way. In other words, they have concerns, needs, or motivations that influence how they feel. As Figure 6 illustrates, while the nature of the conflict is important, it is the motives, needs, or concerns that underlie the conflict that must be surfaced.

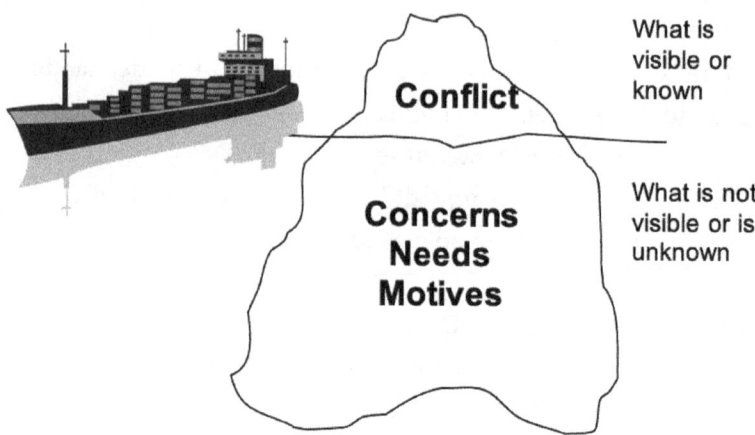

Figure 6: Conflict–Concerns Iceberg

Once Randy and Tara have come to an agreement regarding what they each view as the conflict, they are ready to continue strengthening the working relationship by sharing their motives, needs, or concerns. Tara has expressed a concern that she felt Randy's actions made her look like she did not know what she was doing in front of a customer. If Randy simply tells Tara what to do the next time she has a question, this inner concern is not addressed. Let's see how this conversation might continue with Randy and Tara making their concerns or motives explicit.

Randy explains, "Yeah, I was just in a hurry to get back to stocking the shipment of drugs that had come in and assumed it would be faster for me to show you how to answer this question than explain it. I want you to know that I did not intend to make you look stupid in front of a customer. That was my mistake."

"Well, I guess I overreacted," Tara concedes.

"Listen," Randy continues, "I would like to try to make sure this does not happen again. Can you help me understand how you feel about what happened?"

"Yeah," Tara replies. "At the last store I worked at, there was a more experienced employee that really seemed to feel good about making other employees look bad. It's one of the reasons I left. I just had this bad feeling you were doing the same." Tara explains, "Plus, I am afraid the customer might see me as not knowing what I'm doing, and not seek out my help the next time she comes in the store."

As you can see, this simple but thoughtful conversation can achieve a great deal toward turning what might have been a major conflict into an opportunity for Randy and Tara to build trust in their working relationship. Both Randy and Tara have expressed concerns that are perfectly reasonable but were unknown to each other. Randy was in a hurry to finish stocking and thought it would be faster to show Tara how to complete the sale than to explain it verbally. Tara was concerned that she would not be viewed as competent by the customer.

By going beyond the surface reason for the conflict and striving to understand each other's concerns, needs, or motives, Randy and Tara can determine why the surface conflict matters to each of them so much. In *The Seven Habits of Highly Effective People*, Stephen Covey calls this step, "Seeking first to understand before trying to be understood." Often, individuals in conflict try to resolve the issue while conducting their conversation at a very shallow level. The result is each person presents their personal view on the conflict without trying to understand the reasoning or motivations behind the other person's position. Without understanding the driving needs behind a particular position, we cannot reach a constructive understanding. When a person consistently uses positive communication skills to ensure they understand another's concerns, they build up a deeper level of trust with the other person.

A Word of Caution

It is important to realize that when one takes time to truly understanding another person's reasoning, motives, and concerns, one might find that their suggestion or issue is better than their own, or that different views or ideas can be combined for an even more synergistic solution. Thus, the conflict may lead to a better solution than you or the other party might have developed independently. This is a great example of functional or cooperative conflict, and you should celebrate this when it occurs.

In addition, people's personalities can be very different. While some people feel very comfortable sharing their innermost motivations and needs, others believe it is best to keep all their cards "close to their chest." Some people feel confident in sharing their thoughts and opinions, while others are shy and find it difficult to "bare their soul." Additionally, just because you understand *your* needs and concerns doesn't mean others have given *their* needs and concerns much thought. Again, it is an understandable human tendency to leap directly from problem identification to solution. Others may be embarrassed to reveal what their needs and reasoning might be. In short, it may be necessary to wait and discuss each other's concerns at an appropriate time, or to meet several times before enough trust is created so that you can both engage in an open conversation.

Step 3: Identify Your Goals

Once the other person's concerns, motivations, and needs are understood, it is appropriate to move to the third step in the conflict-mediation process—goal setting. At this point you can explain your goals and clarify the goals of all other parties. The desired outcome of this step is to make everyone's goals explicit and understood. It does not mean you agree with each other's goals, but you do understand them. By making goals explicit, it is easier to sort through them and achieve a "win-win" solution with the other person. Let's pick up the conversation between Randy and Tara to see how this step might be enacted. Tara has explained her experience at the last place she worked.

"That would really make me mad too," agrees Randy. "I want you to know how important I think it is that we work well together so that our customers get good service and you are confident that I am never going to try to make you look bad. I want us all to be successful."

"That sounds reasonable to me, Randy," Tara replies. "I want to work well with you too."

Randy and Tara now have made their goals clear to each other; they are one step closer to resolving the conflict. Both have expressed goals of working well together and ensuring that they can trust each other. It might also be important to connect the goals of the individuals to the higher-level goals of the organization and the standards for guiding behavior and conduct. For example, either Randy or Tara could observe that Apex Drug Store expects that all employees will work collaboratively with each other, respect each other's customers, and present a positive face to all customers. Having two or more employees who distrust or resent each other is not conducive to a positive, productive customer-service environment. It is easy to imagine the negative outcomes that could occur if employees are not communicating and cooperating effectively. This could include over or undercharging for a prescription, filling a prescription incorrectly, filing insurance claims incorrectly, or simply giving customers a bad impression.

Step 4: Action Plan

Once the people in conflict have come to an agreement about the nature of the conflict, clarified their needs, motives, or concerns, and expressed their goals, it is appropriate to develop a plan for action. Clarifying each other's desired actions is beneficial because even when we have the same goal, there may be more than one way of achieving that goal. For example, you and I might agree that we both want to visit New Orleans but have very different ideas about when to go, how to get there, where to stay, and what to do once we arrive. Let's see how Randy and Tara might discuss actions for addressing their conflict:

"So, what can we do next time to ensure that we don't repeat this again?" asked Tara.

"I will try to remember to explain things or at least check to see what type of assistance you want me to provide," said Randy. "But I would also like you to try and make it clear what help you want from me, just in case."

"Fair enough," said Tara. "But something else occurs to me. I have been so busy just learning the pricing and inventory for this store, I will bet there are other procedures I don't know, but I have not even had a chance to discover what those might be. Suppose you and I sit down when we have time and review all the procedures one at a time. You can help me understand them. Would that work for you?"

"It would be a pleasure. Plus, if you have any good ideas which you learned at your last job, I would be glad to learn any new techniques."

What could have been a very unpleasant situation has now been turned into an opportunity for continued growth and cooperation. Sometimes, people resist following the CCGA process because they think it will take too long. As you can see from the example above, it really does not have to take a long time at all. The conversation above would have taken no more than two to three minutes. Imagine how much time and energy could have been wasted if Tara and Randy had simply let the situation decay. Can you imagine the misunderstandings and conflicts occurring in your healthcare organization that you could turn into productive, positive, respectful experiences between people?

In this situation, the actions defined were relatively simple. In other conflicts, it might be necessary to develop much more detailed action plans that describe who will do what, by when, with what resources or support, and with what outcomes or key measures.

FOLLOW the CCGA CYCLE

We highly recommend that you follow the cycle of identifying the conflict, sharing concerns and needs, clarifying goals, and developing an action plan. There are several reasons for this. First, our natural tendency when presented with a problem or conflict is to jump from identifying the conflict to taking action. After all, we are problem solvers, we have things to do, so we want to take action and get on with life. While this is fast, it is not effective for most conflicts. If you do not take time to understand needs, concerns, and motivations, you are simply identifying the surface issue and ignoring the underlying emotions and feelings behind the conflict. This is like cutting off the top of an iceberg and ignoring the reality that the rest of the iceberg is just going to float to the surface. Thus, if you are constantly "solving conflicts" where you work only to see them surface again and again, you are most likely not getting to the reasons for the conflict in the first place.

The second reason it is important to follow the CCGA process is that being *heard* is a critical need everyone shares in a conversation. We all have reasons for the positions or perspectives we hold. Taking time to genuinely listen to why someone feels the way they do demonstrates care, concern, and empathy. This is a very important step in the process of building trust, confidence, and a culture of openness.

DIAGRAMMING the CONFLICT, CONCERNS, GOALS, ACTION (CCGA) PROCESS

While many conflicts can be resolved as simply as in the case of Randy and Tara, other conflicts are more complex. In these cases, we find that it is beneficial to diagram or describe the various steps of the CCGA process in written form. The advantage of diagramming the conflict is twofold. First, the mapping process provides you with a means of thinking through a potential conflict before confronting someone. Second, by diagramming a conflict on a piece of paper, a whiteboard, or flipchart, the problem-solving and thought process is transparent to all involved. Let's look at an example to see how this might be accomplished.

CASE STUDY #1: ROMANTIC NIGHT OUT

This case example concerns a married couple, and while you may not be married, you should be able to identify with one or both of the individuals involved. As you read the case, see if you can identify what each person might view as the conflict; their individual needs, motivations, or concerns; goals; and what possible actions might be taken.

Rebecca has been working late every night this week. It's Friday evening, and she is looking forward to relaxing at home. In fact, Rebecca picked up a video that she thinks will be perfect just to sit back and calm down. As she enters the door, her husband, Thomas, greets her with the following news. "Honey, guess what? I made reservations for us to go out to dinner tonight, and I bought tickets to the concert you want to see. The babysitter will be here in just a few minutes, so you need to shower and change quickly or we will miss our dinner reservations."

Take a few minutes to fill in the blanks for each of the CCGA process steps below. There is no right or wrong answer. You may find that you need to view the conflict from Thomas's point of view, and then go back and do the same from Rebecca's point of view.

1. What is the conflict?
Thomas:_____
Rebecca:_____
2. What might be each person's concerns?
Thomas:_____
Rebecca:_____
3. What might be each person's goals?
Thomas:_____
Rebecca:_____
4. What actions might meet each person's goals?
Thomas:_____
Rebecca:_____

Figure 6 illustrates how this case might be diagrammed in

order to make the entire CCGA process explicit. Recognize that the responses listed in the visual diagram below (Figure 7) are not the only ways this case might be illustrated. You may very well have come up with observations for Thomas and Rebecca that are just as relevant as those depicted.

Figure 7: Romantic Night Out CCGA Diagram

What is the conflict?

You might notice what your reaction was when you first read the case. For many, this is no conflict at all. We often have participants in our workshops say, "Wow, if my spouse (or partner) did this for me, I would *drag* myself along no matter how tired I was!" On the other hand, some observe, "This sounds just like my spouse (or partner). They want to go out all the time. I get so tired of feeling like we have to go out night after night, and frankly, we can't afford it!" And occasionally someone might observe, "Thomas must have *really* done something wrong and is trying to make up for it." Again, you get the idea that one's previous experiences, expectations, and perceptions have a great deal to do with how one views a potential conflict. Therefore, while some readers may not view this situation as very serious, if not handled with tact and care, it could become a much bigger issue.

The reason we ask you to consider your reaction to the case is to illustrate how easy it is for each of us to interpret what is going on and to assign meaning to what goes on around us or what we observe. This also illustrates that we each have our own perspective on a situation, and that perspective dramatically influences how we feel about the conflict.

We recommend trying to sum up the conflict in the simplest possible terms. As the visual diagram above depicts, Thomas and Rebecca see the conflict from two different perspectives. Rebecca would like to stay home, and Thomas would like to go out.

What are each person's concerns?

Rebecca has had a hard week. She is tired, worn out, and needs time to unwind. For all we know, she also has a lot to do the next day and would like to get to bed early. On the other hand, it appears that Thomas is trying to do something nice for the both of them. He may know that Rebecca particularly likes the restaurant and certainly knows she wanted to attend the concert. He may also recognize that the two of them don't get to go out very often and is proud of himself for taking the initiative to get this "date" all set up—including a sitter.

What might be each person's goals?

Rebecca would probably prefer to stay at home and do nothing. She might want Thomas to cancel the sitter, reservations, and exchange the tickets for another date. We can also presume she wants to maintain a positive relationship with Thomas. We can also surmise that Thomas is all set to go out and have some fun anyway, but he also wants to maintain a positive relationship with Rebecca.

What actions might meet each person's goals?

If unproductive conflict is their goal, Rebecca could say, "Oh, *alright*, I'll go, but I don't want to!" If so, she may go out and resent every minute. Of course, Thomas could reply, "Oh great! I finally try to do something nice for us, and all you want to do is stay at home. I'll cancel everything and we'll just sit here and do nothing!"

There are also quite a number of positive options to resolve this conflict. It may be possible for Thomas to cancel all the plans and reschedule for another weekend. On the other hand, the tickets to the concert may be nonrefundable, in which case Thomas could cancel the dinner reservations and allow Rebecca time to relax a little before they go out. Rebecca may decide that after taking a quick shower and getting something to eat, she feels reenergized and ready to go out after all. Rebecca and Thomas may decide that he should cancel the dinner reservations and simply go to the concert by himself or with a friend. Note that there are many ways to resolve the conflict. Which one is best for this couple is dependent on their relationship and ability to work constructively with each other.

CASE STUDY #2: WORK TEAM

Let's try another case example between two members in a healthcare working environment. Read through the case below and see if you can identify what the conflict, concerns, goals, and actions might be for Julia, Ted, *and* the work team.

Julia and Ted are team members working in the same nursing home. One day they are gathered with the rest of the team at the morning meeting to discuss the patients, the care each is receiving, and other issues related to care. At one point in the meeting, the team leader points out that spring break is coming up soon and that there may be an influx of visitors during that period.

Julia speaks up and says, "Oh yeah, thanks for bringing this up. I want to remind everyone that I am taking the week of spring break off for vacation."

"Yeah, me too," says Ted.

One of the team members says, "Remember that last year we agreed as a group that we can't have two people out on vacation during the same time period. If we do, our ability to provide effective patient care could be a problem."

Julia shrugs. "Look, I have two kids in grade school and they are off all week, so I have to take those days off. I don't get to see my kids enough anyway, and it's the only time I can spend some quality time with them."

"Well, I haven't taken a vacation all year," says Ted. "I'm going to technical school at night and this is the only time that I have a week off."

"Well, I spoke up first, so I get to go," Julia replies.

"That's not fair, Julia," says Ted, "Schools have other holidays you can take off."

"Yeah," Julia observes. "But not a whole week, just a day or so here and there at the end of a weekend. How come you need a whole week?"

"My parents live in Ohio and it takes longer for me to get there. I haven't been home to see my family for three years," Ted says. "You still get to spend time with your kids every weekend."

Julia shakes her head. "Sorry, I understand, but I'm a single mom. I can't afford to pay for childcare for a whole week while I work. And think about it. Do you think my kids will enjoy their vacation if they spend the entire time in childcare or with a babysitter? Sorry, but I spoke up first, so I'm taking vacation."

"Well," Ted states, "I'm not waiting another year to see my parents. Besides, it's a stupid rule that two people can't take vacation at the same time."

1. What is the conflict?

Julia:_____

Ted:_____

Work Team:_____

2. What might be each person's concerns?

Julia:_____

Ted:_____

Work Team:_____

3. What might be each person's goals?

Julia:_____

Ted:_____

Work Team:_____

4. What actions might meet each person's goals?

Julia:_____

Ted:_____

Work Team:_____

Work Team:
- Investigate validity of "two out" rule
- Hire a temp
- Other members work overtime or cover while both go on vacation
- First who spoke goes
- Split the week between Ian and Julia
- One goes this time, the other gets priority next time
- Flip a coin

Julia:
- See if she can work ahead
- Work half days
- Split week with Ted

Ted:
- See if he can work ahead

Conflict (Surface Problem)
Julia: Go on vacation
Ted: Go on vacation
Work Team: Vacation sign-up not clear

Actions (Who, what, when...)

Communication Skills

Concerns (Motives, needs)
Julia: Single mom, expense, school vacation, quality time with kids
Ted: School vacation, has not seen parents
Work Team: Production, maintain good team relationships, follow policy, fairness

Goals (Win-win solution)
Julia: Go on vacation, spend quality time with kid, avoid excessive expenses
Ted: Go on vacation, see parents
Work Team: Maintain production, support both team members, fairness

Figure 8: Vacation Day CCGA Diagram

At first glance, this may appear to be just a conflict between Julia and Ted, but it really involves the entire team since patient care is involved.

What is the conflict?

As depicted above, both Julia and Ted probably view the conflict as wanting to take vacation at the same time. This is also a conflict for the team because the vacation policy does not appear to be clear (is there advanced sign-up, is it first come first served, etc.). The team must also be concerned with patient care. The conflict is important to all involved because it will set a precedent if and when this situation occurs again in the future.

What are the concerns?

Note that Julia, Ted, and the team members all have very legitimate concerns or needs. Being a single mom, Julia is concerned that she needs to spend time with her children over spring break and avoid any major expenses for daycare. Ted wants to see his family and, given the distance, argues that he needs the full spring break period to make the visit. The work team must maintain patient care, but also wants to be fair to both Julia and Ted while following company policy. We might also assume that Julia and Ted are interested in the work team maintaining good patient care since their pay and concern for their patients they care for every day may be affected.

What are the goals?

Both Julia and Ted would prefer to go on vacation. Further, Julia would like to avoid any unnecessary expenses. The work team has the goal of maintaining patient care, being fair, but also supporting both individuals' need to go on vacation.

What are some possible actions?

As with the case we looked at with Thomas and Rebecca, there may be any number of possible actions which could address this situation. Following are just a few suggestions:

1. One person goes now, and the other goes the following week or gets to go during spring break next year. In the real world,

there may be excellent reasons why there is a policy that only one person can go on vacation at one time. After all, don't forget that the team originally developed the policy as a group; they must have had a good reason. The bottom line is that the decision that only one person gets to go on vacation at a time may still be the best for the whole team. Guaranteeing that the other person gets to go on vacation later may be the best solution the team can offer.

2. Hire a temporary worker or have team members work overtime. It may be worth checking to see if funds are available to hire a temporary worker or have another team member work overtime to ensure the right level of patient care. Depending on the level of team autonomy, the team may be able to make this decision, or it may need to negotiate this possibility with management. Maybe this issue has occurred at a time when other team members can cover the absence of two members during regular work hours.

3. Revisit the rule. After considering all the options, the team may find that while the rule made sense in the past, it does not make sense now. Or, after looking at the facts, the team may find that at certain times of the year, the rule makes sense, but during other times, it does not.

4. Julia and Ted might both take vacation during spring break, but not the full week. Julia and Ted may decide that to maintain good relations and ensure quality patient care, they will each take a few days off at different times during the week.

5. Other options?

As you can see from these two case examples, the CCGA process is a very simple yet powerful method for identifying the key elements that influence the resolution of a potential conflict. Taking the time to clearly understand what a problem looks like from another's perspective, why the other person feels the way they do, what a good solution might look like, and what actions might be taken to resolve the problem helps those involved maintain a high level of trust and solve problems in a cooperative spirit.

An important aspect of this process that you should keep in mind is that the ability to resolve conflict is heavily influenced by the relationship between the people involved. The more trust and the more effective the level of communication, the higher the probability that a positive solution will be achieved. When high levels of trust and a positive relationship exist, a conflict can likely be resolved by moving sequentially through the four process steps.

If a conflict is particularly difficult, or trust is very low, the people involved may need to work through the CCGA cycle a number of times before reaching a resolution. This may involve reaching small agreements, building trust, improving communication, reaching another small agreement, building trust, and so on until a successful resolution is reached. It is also important to give people time to reflect on progress, information shared, and to gain control of emotions. For example, if during the course of a conflict-mediation or problem-solving session you share information that the other party needs to verify or reflect upon, then both parties may agree to adjourn and regroup later. Similarly, if emotions get out of control, it may be wise to take a break and return to the discussion when cooler heads prevail.

In chapter four, you will learn specific communication skills that can be used at each stage of the CCGA model to enhance communication.

> ***The Least You Need to Remember***
> - Your chances of advancing in your career are enhanced if you can address conflict effectively.
> - Addressing conflict means having all parties agree on the conflict, share their concerns, discuss goals, and develop an action plan.
> - Conflict can be dealt with effectively if you visually map or diagram the conflict using the CCGA process.

CHAPTER 3 TOOLS AND ACTIVITIES

In this activity you will map out a conflict you are facing. A graphic of the CCGA process is provided. As in the examples you have read in this chapter, it is suggested that you follow this procedure:

1. Take a few minutes to identify a conflict in which you are now involved. This could be a conflict at work, or with a family member or friend.
2. List yourself and the other parties.
3. Identify what each person might view as the conflict. (You are not agreeing on how you will resolve the problem; you are just agreeing on the surface conflict.)
4. Complete the concerns, goals, and actions blocks for yourself.
5. Complete the concerns, goals, and action blocks for the other persons. Try to be objective and honestly reflect what you believe the other person might say and feel.

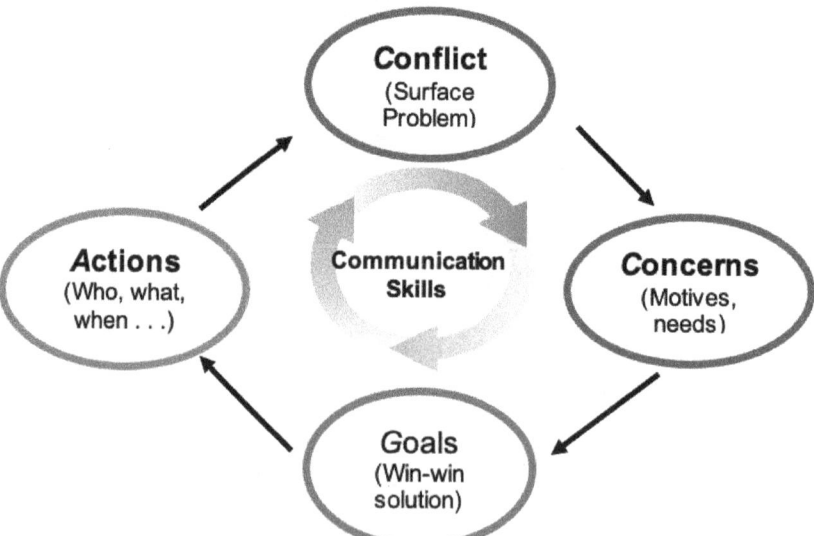

6. Look at the information you have completed to determine the following:

- Do all parties view the conflict the same? If not, why do you think they might see it differently?
- Are you able to understand the other person's concerns or goals better?
- What goals does each prefer? Are there areas of overlap from which you might collaborate to develop a "win-win" solution?
- What actions can you all agree upon to resolve the conflict?

Chapter 4
COMMUNICATION SKILLS

> *We have used rules and regulations . . .*
> *to make ourselves safe. But there is no safety*
> *in separation. We find well-being only when we*
> *remember that we belong together.*
> —M. Wheatley and M. Kellner-Rogers

In This Chapter

Thus far, you have learned that conflict can be addressed most constructively if individuals and organizations share common standards for guiding conduct and behavior, and follow a process that ensures that all parties are heard. In this chapter, we will examine communication skills that serve as the third element of the conflict-mediation system. You will learn that effective communication goes well beyond simply telling someone what you think. Rather, truly effective communication ensures that both you and the individual with whom you are communicating are able to share your thoughts and feelings, while feeling equally confident that you have been fully heard.

Communication is the glue that holds organizations and individuals together. When employees and management communicate openly and effectively, they are able to accomplish individual and organizational goals, implement and respond to changes, coordinate activities, and engage in actions that enhance success. Experts in the field of communication observe that effective communication is the result of a common understanding between the communicator and the receiver. In fact, the word *communication* comes from the Latin word *communis*, meaning "common." In essence, the person speaking is trying to establish a common understanding with the person receiving the message. If the communicator and receiver are not able to communicate to achieve a common understanding, mistakes, misunderstandings, and conflict frequently occur.

So far, you have learned about two of the three foundations of the conflict-mediation system. The first leg is the need to establish standards for guiding conduct and behavior. The second leg is to train all employees in the process for mediating conflicts. Developing strong, collaborative communication skills is the third aspect for enhancing organizational success. Communicating clearly through conflict requires the ability to tactfully and respectfully confront the conflict openly, listen to others, acknowledge what we have heard, respond effectively, and then commit to some action. We will refer to these five elements by the acronym *CLARC*—for Confront, Listen, Acknowledge, Respond, and Commit.

CONFRONT

Most conflicts escalate because people do not address problems openly and honestly. Instead, many people avoid conflict and simply allow a problem to grow until it becomes a major issue. Others accommodate or compromise in ways that seem appropriate for the short term, but with which they become dissatisfied over the long term. Some people use a competitive approach to get their way through force of personality, position, or threats. This latter approach can be thought of an "I win–you lose" outcome that usually results in a situation that one party strongly resents. If the ultimate result is that one or more individuals fail to fully support the decision, the conflict will usually fester and need to be addressed again later.

In the business environment, conflicts that continually resurrect themselves are generally a recipe for poor customer service, lowered productivity or efficiency, and declining interpersonal relationships. The only way to consistently achieve positive, constructive results over the long term is by collaborating to identify and resolve current or potential conflicts. The only way to get this process started is to confront the issue respectfully.

Confrontation is one of those words that can have more than one meaning. Confrontation is most commonly used or interpreted by people in a negative manner. When used in a negative manner, confrontation conveys a hostile or defiant position. Confrontation as we use the word means the people involved openly recognize and bring a problem or issue forward to be examined collaboratively. The intent is *not* to throw the problem or issue in the face of the other party involved. Rather, the purpose is to make the problem, opportunity, or issue explicit or observable to everyone.

The goal of the confrontation step is to be appropriately assertive. Appropriate assertiveness allows you to state your case without arousing the defenses of the other person. You are appropriately assertive when you begin by explaining how you perceive a situation rather than telling the other person what they should or should not do. The best method we have found for confronting a problem or issue between individuals or teams is to use "I" statements. The purpose of "I" statements is to ensure that the person who is confronting the other person takes ownership of their feelings in a nonthreatening fashion. "I" statements allow you to express your ideas and opinions without blaming or attacking the other person.

Use an "I" statement when you need to let the other person know that you feel strongly about the issue. Others can underestimate how hurt, angry, or put out you are, so it's useful to say exactly what's going on for you—describing, not blaming. Your "I" statement should be simple and clear. A complete "I" statement includes four crucial elements (Figure 9):

Four Elements of an "I" Statement	How to State these Elements
1. A description of the situation or behavior 2. Your personal reaction or feelings 3. The consequences from your perspective 4. A query on how the other party views this issue	1. When (describe the situation or behavior), 2. I feel (state your personal reaction or feeling) 3. Because (describe the consequences) 4. I'd like to hear how you feel about this issue, what you think, etc.

Figure 9: "I" Statements

For example, suppose a coworker is frequently late for work and you have to cover for them until they arrive. One way to respond might be to say, "Hey look, I'm tired of you coming in late all the time, so you better be on time tomorrow!" Even if you are correct, the other person will probably react defensively. You can confront the other member in a more positive manner using an "I" statement such as "When you are late for work, I feel irritated because I have to do my job and your job, and the quality of both suffers. How do you see this situation?"

Consider another example. James is a lab technician working on a project with several other individuals. One day he is focusing intently on transferring some volatile chemicals to a storage rack when a colleague says, "Hey, James, stop whatever you are doing and get me those pipettes right now." James continues concentrating on putting up the chemicals and says, "As soon as I get these chemicals put away safely." His colleague yells, "No, stop whatever you are doing and get me those pipettes NOW!"

If you are like most people, your response might be to withdraw rapidly (maybe slamming the door on the way out), or responding, "Get it yourself!" Resist the temptation to shout back to stop the onslaught, and deal with your rising anger.

This is the time for being appropriately assertive. James takes a deep breath and responds:

"When I hear someone talk to me that way, it makes me feel disrespected and humiliated because it does not make me feel like my priorities matter. I'd like to discuss this with you so that we understand each other and can work together effectively."

As you can see, by using an "I" statement, you clearly identify the issue, how you feel, and what you think the consequences might be from your perspective. This has been achieved in a positive fashion that also allows the other individual to respond. Using an "I" statement is also a great way to start the CCGA process by letting the other person know you have a concern and an indication of what your needs might be; e.g., "I need to focus on doing my work so that the quality does not suffer." Also, notice that using an "I" statement is not intended to be "weak," but at the same time is not rude. It is simply intended to be a clear opening to the conversation. Do not expect the "I" statement to fix things straightaway or that the other person is going to respond as you want them to immediately.

A well-intentioned "I" statement is
- unlikely to do any harm
- a step in the right direction
- sure to change the current situation in some way
- open to possibilities that you may not yet see

Now that we have discussed how to confront an issue, we are ready to look at the skill of listening.

LISTEN

For quality communication to take place, it is important that the parties involved listen to each other. Effective listening is a lot more than just avoiding the bad habits of interrupting someone or trying to finish their sentences when they are speaking.

Effective listening also means taking the time to pay attention to what the other person is saying so that you also understand what that person feels and wants. It means listening for their reasons, experiences, and assumptions so that you understand what thoughts are driving their comments or recommendations. Effective listening stems from being patient enough to listen to the other person's entire train of thought rather than waiting impatiently for your chance to respond.

Careful listening is difficult when you have different ideas from others. If you react too quickly to come to a judgment without taking time to understand the other person, the chance for defensiveness increases greatly. You want to understand the other person first, but understanding someone does not necessarily mean that you accept their point of view.

When you encounter a different view from your own, follow three simple rules: delay judgment, pay attention to the whole meaning of what is being said, and ask questions to ensure you understand what is being said.

DELAY JUDGEMENT

Delaying judgment means that you should not be too quick to criticize the other person—even in your own head. In the bestseller *Don't Sweat the Small Stuff . . . and It's All Small Stuff*, Richard Carlson observes that when you hurry someone along, interrupt, or finish another person's sentences, you must keep track not only of your own thoughts, but those of the person you are interrupting.

Carlson goes on to note that this style of ineffective listening makes people nervous and leads to arguments and resentment. If there is anything that really bothers people, it's trying to explain something to another person who is not listening to what you are saying. On the other hand, we all appreciate those individuals who we feel always take the time to really listen. To build a strong, effective team-communication process, each team member must, as Stephen Covey points out, seek first to understand, then to be understood.

PAY ATTENTION

The second aspect of listening is to pay attention to the entire meaning of the message. Try to go beyond simply catching the facts being discussed and sense the concerns behind what the other individual is expressing. What are the feelings, reasoning, needs, and assumptions behind the other person's comments? What are the implications of what is being said not only for the other person, but for you and the rest of the work group? To listen effectively, you must consciously slow down your thinking and wait for the other person to finish. It also means that you should pay attention to the other person's body language and tone of speech. People often convey a great deal about their feelings or attitudes by the tone of voice, their posture, and/or the gestures they use during a conversation.

Finally, ask questions to ensure you understand what is being said. The philosophy behind this point should not be missed: people almost always have good reasons for their opinions or point of view. Even if you disagree with the other person's opinion or point of view, they will respond much more positively to you if you convey to them that you appreciate and understand what they are saying.

When the other individual has completed their point, try to find out as much as you can about their perspective by asking nonjudgmental questions. For example, ask them questions that allow them to clarify:
- What happened?
- Who was involved?
- How were they personally affected?
- What do they hope to achieve for themselves and for the team with their suggestion?

People have been raised differently, have had different

experiences, and approach life differently. Asking nonjudgmental questions as suggested above allows you to understand how others might come to different conclusions than you. Once you feel that you understand both the content and reasoning behind what another person is saying, you can then acknowledge what you believe you have heard.

ACKNOWLEDGE

Effective communication is a process of both sending a message and ensuring that it is properly received. It is generally not enough to simply hear what another person is saying.

You may have played the children's game called "Telephone." In the game, one person tells the next person in line a short message. The second person then repeats the message to the third person and so on until all children involved have "heard" and passed on the message. The result is usually that the original and final messages have very little in common. The reason is that each person hears, interprets, and rewords the message slightly differently from the person that conveyed the message to them.

Similarly, for other people to feel that you have truly heard what they have to say, you must accurately acknowledge what you believe they said. Further, they must agree that you heard them correctly. There are a number of productive ways to acknowledge what another person said. One way is to restate what the other person has said. A few examples of effective use of restating are illustrated in Figure 10.

What to Restate	Example
Main points the other person has made	"So your biggest concern is making sure everyone has an important role on our team?"
Important details raised	"You're saying that next year's budget allows us to increase our recognition fund by 10 percent?"
Comments that might help move the conversation forward	"It sounds like you are suggesting we put partitions on the manufacturing floor to provide a quiet place for team members to meet. Is that right?"
Information you might not have understood	"I'm not clear—do you want to attend the training session on Tuesday or Thursday afternoon?"
Comments or suggestions when you think the other person might not feel they were understood	"Jean, did you just say that we are due for a quality improvement audit next month?"

Figure 10: Restatement Examples

You can also acknowledge what another person has said in a constructive manner by reframing. Reframing helps to soften and neutralize hostile comments and encourages forward movement by clarifying thoughts or introducing creative possibilities. Some examples of reframing are illustrated in Figure 11.

What to reframe	Example
From past to future	A team member says, "I am getting sick and tired of all these absences! We can't get any work done!" **Reframe**: "So you want to see attendance improved in the future, is that right?"
From negative to positive	A coworker says, "This twelve-hour shift is too much." **Reframe**: "It sounds like you want to find a way to make the work shift more tolerable."
From personal attack to problem definition	An employee says, "If that secretary forgets to give me my messages one more time I am going to scream." **Reframe**: "Are you saying that we need to find a better method of ensuring messages get passed along?"
From a demand to a goal	A coworker says, "I want a private office so I can get away from all these distractions!" **Reframe**: "You need a way to get your work done without distractions?"
From an individual concern to a team concern	A team member says, "I had so much to do I couldn't monitor the equipment until after 3 PM." **Reframe**: "It sounds like we need to work out a way to make sure someone can monitor the equipment on a regular basis."
From a concern to an action	A manager says, "We waste too much time in these meetings and nothing gets done." **Reframe**: "Are you suggesting that it might help if we have an agenda for each meeting?"

Figure 11: Reframing Examples

These are just a few suggestions for ensuring that you acknowledge what another person has said in a way that allows them to correct you if needed. By acknowledging in this manner, you can ensure that what you thought you heard is what the other person really said.

RESPOND

The CLARC skills you have learned so far include how to confront the other person to make a problem or issue explicit in a way that does not cause a defensive reaction. You have also learned how to listen so that the other person feels he or she has your attention. Third, you have learned how to acknowledge what you have heard. Again, you are not agreeing with the other person but simply ensuring that what was said is what you heard.

The fourth of the CLARC skills is to respond. One can respond in two different ways. First, you can respond to gather additional information and to better understand perspectives, feelings, concerns, or needs. Second, you may respond to give your reply, answer, or reaction to what the other person is saying.

Ideally, when you respond to someone, do so in a way that allows for a common, open, and free exchange of ideas and thoughts so that you are able to build the conversation in a positive way. You should avoid responding to someone in a way that closes the door on the discussion or "puts down" what was said. For example, giving a flat response of "no" closes the door on a conversation. Saying, "Yes, but . . ." is a negative response as you are saying, "Yes, I heard you, but I don't agree." This is the same thing as saying "no."

To encourage additional information, perspective, feelings, or concerns, it is better to respond in a way that conveys that you are open-minded, respectful, and willing to explore options. Ask open-ended questions that request additional information, a different perspective, exploration of alternatives, and so on. Figure 12 lists a number of ways that you can respond to encourage the conversation.

1. What would it look like if . . . ?
2. What would have to happen to make your suggestion possible?
3. What would need to change . . . ?
4. Who is a good model of . . . ?
5. What works best when . . . ?
6. Can you tell me about a time when what you are suggesting went just right?
7. What have we done that has worked well before?
8. How do you think this decision affects the team (or another unit)?

Figure 12: Responding Examples

These responses are just examples, of course. You can modify them or add any other similar type of response that helps to foster effective communication.

For example, let's say that another employee approaches you and says, "I am so tired of trying to work with Bob. I asked him three times where this file we have been working on is, and he continued to look out the window as if I wasn't even there!"

One way to respond might be to say, "Yes, isn't he a loser?" Doing so, however, does not build the strength of the group or resolve this situation. A better response might be to say, "What have you done in the past that was successful at getting Bob's attention?" Or, "Really? That does not sound like Bob. What do you think must be going on for him to be in such a thoughtful mood?"

Something to consider is that if you respond in a negative manner about another person, the individual with whom you are speaking may wonder what you say about them when they are not around.

The second way to respond is to share your reaction or feelings about what someone else has suggested. You have already learned one effective method is to use "I" statements. Remember that a good "I" statement identifies what the issue is, how you feel, and what you think the consequences are from your perspective. The purpose of a good "I" statement is to respond in a positive fashion that also allows the other individual to respond in kind.

For example, in a team meeting, someone might suggest a new method for orienting new members to the work environment. You might say, "Ted, if I understood you correctly, you are suggesting that we each spend one hour with each new team member to explain our role on the team. I like that idea because when we take the time to explain what we do to new members, they are able to become fully performing team members sooner." In this example, we combined the acknowledgment skill with a response using an "I" statement.

COMMIT

A major source of conflict between group members occurs when they fail to commit to some action or next steps. Group members should commit when they are satisfied that the present item or suggestion under discussion has been sufficiently covered to move on.

Sometimes individuals begin a discussion, agree on the cause of a conflict or the necessary solution, but stop without defining a next step. When this happens, people may leave with different and perhaps contradictory ideas of what a solution might be, when it might happen, and who will address the problem. Worse yet, if someone leaves the discussion feeling that their interests or needs are not fully understood, they may sabotage the effort in some way.

To avoid a conflict due to lack of commitment, it is important to clarify who, what, when, where, how, and why.

- By defining *who*, the team is ensuring that accountability is clear.
- By discussing *what*, you are clarifying the actual action or steps the individual who is accountable will take.
- *When* defines the period within which the action or steps will be taken.

- *Where*, if appropriate, makes the physical location or setting explicit.
- By defining *how*, you are identifying any resource or procedural needs or limitations.
- Finally, explaining *why* ensures that the reason for investing the time and energy is clear.

In the last chapter, you read the case example in which Thomas had "surprised" Rebecca by buying tickets to a concert, getting a babysitter, and offering to take her out to dinner. After working through the CCGA process, the commitment step might look something like this:

Thomas: "I can see where you might have been happier if I had called and told you about the concert tonight, but I was trying to surprise you."

Rebecca: "Yeah, but I really appreciate what you did. That was thoughtful. Look, let me go take a shower and change. You cancel the dinner reservations and order pizza. We can take our time, relax, and get to the concert in plenty of time that way, and I don't have to rush around."

Thomas: "Sounds good. I'll come tell you when the pizza gets here."

APPLYING the CLARC SKILLS

Knowing the CLARC skills is one thing; using them on a daily basis and when you are in a conflict is another. As indicated at the beginning of this chapter, any skill or combination of skills should be used when appropriate. When trying to resolve a conflict, it may be necessary to confront the problem, listen to what the other person has to say, acknowledge, listen more, respond, listen more, respond, acknowledge, and respond again before you ever reach the commitment stage. Don't be surprised if you revisit a skill several times during the course of a conversation.

> ### *The Least You Need to Remember*
>
> - It is important to confront a conflict openly, honestly, and in a manner that does not cause undue defensiveness.
> - "I" statements are a wonderful technique for confronting conflict.
> - Listening means taking time to truly hear what the other person says and feels.
> - When you acknowledge what someone has said, you are ensuring you heard it correctly.
> - Responding allows you to gather additional information or share your reply.
> - Commitment includes defining who will do what, when, where, how, why, etc.

CHAPTER 4 TOOLS and ACTIVITIES

Personal Communication Skills Inventory

The table below lists the five aspects of communication that comprise the CLARC skills. For each list note whether you need to perform this skill more or less often, and how you plan on taking action to improve.

Skill	Need to Do Better or More Often	Action Plan for Improvement
Confront		
Listen		
Acknowledge		
Respond		
Commit		

Organizational Communication Skills Audit

Good communication is vital to the effective operations of any organization. This Organizational Communication Skills Audit will help you understand how effective your organization is at optimizing its internal communications.

Listed below are ten questions. Look at each and place an *X* in the appropriate response.

Item	Strongly Disagree	Disagree	Neutral	Agree	Strongly Agree
In our organization, we are careful to focus on the problem, not the person.					
All employees have been trained to communicate effectively.					
We listen patiently and respectfully to each other.					
We are able to express our views to anyone without feeling defensive.					
When we face conflict, everyone is careful to understand each other's motives and feelings.					
Employees feel comfortable communicating between different levels of management.					
We never attack or ridicule others during meetings.					
Management clearly communicates expectations so that conflict is avoided.					
We take time to periodically assess and improve our ability to communicate.					
Management takes time to listen to and respond to our ideas and suggestions for improvement.					
Total # Xs					

Scoring:
1. Enter the number of *X*s you entered in each column
2. Multiply as indicted:
    a. Number of Xs in *Strongly Disa*gree x 5   = _____
    b. Number of Xs in *Disagree* x 4   = _____
    c. Number of Xs in *Neutral* x 3   = _____
    d. Number of Xs in *Agree* x 2   = _____
    e. Number of Xs in *Strongly Agr*ee x 1   = _____
3. Total a + b +c +d + e = _____

Interpretation:

35–50: Your organization is probably experiencing misalignment, conflict, and misunderstandings due to poor communication skills.

21–34: Your organization is moderately effective at communicating internally.

10–20: Your organization demonstrates effective communication skills.

Activities for Building Trust and Understanding

Professional sports teams do not practice once a year and hope to remain in top form. Rather, they practice every day and constantly try to improve. Work groups that are able to communicate and interact effectively to build trusting, effective relationships and attain high-quality outcomes also practice their skills frequently. Following are a few suggested activities you can apply to help build and sustain a high level of competence and communication.

Note: The team may need to appoint or ask for a facilitator to help with these activities.

Preparing for Potential Hot Spots

For this activity, the individuals or work group members address the following concern: "At some point in our working relationship, we may say or do something to another person that they might find offensive, disrespectful, or hurtful."

1. Brainstorm a list of things people might say or do that others would find offensive or hurtful.
2. Discuss why others might inadvertently say or behave this way and why others would find this offensive or hurtful.
3. Discuss how people should respond when this occurs in the future.

Zen Counting

This incredibly simplistic exercise can be quite challenging. It appeals to your company's introverts and other individuals that enjoy thought-provoking interactions.

1. Team or workgroup members sit in a circle facing away from each other.
2. In no particular order, they are instructed to count from one to ten aloud with each member only saying, at most, one number. In other words, at some point, someone has to start by saying, "One." Then someone else has to decide when to

say, "Two" and so on until the group gets to ten.
3. No other words should be spoken. If two or more team members say a number at the same time or forget and repeat a number, the exercise starts back at one.

Note: The healthcare profession can be very stressful, and taking time to listen and relax is not easy. This value of this exercise is that it creates stillness, mindfulness, and teaches team members to find courage in spite of not knowing what will happen next. This also forces them to listen carefully to one another.

"Who's got a dollar?" Exercise

Most people do not have a very good feel for their own personal level of trust. "Who's got a dollar" is a good initial exercise to get team or workgroup members to start thinking about their own personal level of risk-taking and trust. This activity can occur with team or group members sitting in a circle, in small groups, etc.

1. The facilitator stands up and asks the team, "Who's got a dollar?" (Waiting patiently, eventually someone reaches into their pocket or purse and gives the facilitator a dollar bill.)
2. The facilitator then asks the giver, "What kind of a place would you like this company or organization to become that would make you proud to come to work every day?"
3. When the giver has answered the question, the facilitator takes the dollar, walks over to another person, hands him or her the dollar, and asks the same question.
4. Next, the facilitator asks the group, "Who's got a ten-dollar bill?" More fidgeting and up pops a ten-dollar bill. The same question is asked of the giver, and then the facilitator gives the ten-dollar bill to another person and asks the same question of this individual.
5. Now, the facilitator asks, "Who's got a twenty-dollar bill?" Again, the question is asked, and a transfer of money takes place.

6. At this point, the facilitator stops, asks that the money be returned to its rightful owners, and explains the importance of trust to the performance of teams.
7. Questions for the group to discuss:
   - What were the thoughts and feelings the individuals who gave money had about taking a risk and trusting that the money would be returned?
   - Why didn't others give a dollar?
   - How did people feel when the ante was raised to ten or twenty dollars? Did you think the volunteers were foolish? We may not all be as trusting as we thought.
8. The facilitator should lead a discussion that focuses on the following issues:
   - How do group members feel about the hopes and aspirations described? What would they add? What would it take to achieve these hopes and aspirations?
   - How much do group members trust each other?
   - What benefit would everyone gain if trust were enhanced?
   - What can they do to enhance trust individually and as a group?
   - What are they willing to commit to doing?

Chapter 5
COACHING OTHERS EXPERIENCING CONFLICT

> *Whatever fundamental assumption you hold about human nature, it will be validated by the response your behavior will evoke from people around you.*
> —Frederic Laloux

In This Chapter

A common complaint from managers and employees alike is that some individuals avoid taking responsibility for resolving conflicts or challenges that they are fully capable of addressing. In this chapter, you will learn how to coach others who are experiencing conflict. The value of this skill is those in managerial or supervisory roles can help their employees build the skills they need to work constructively with each other and solve problems quickly. This skill is also valuable for all employees as it is a positive and productive means for ensuring that one does not become part of the gossip or rumor chain. Whether you are a manager or employee, the result of applying your coaching skills will be to enhance the quality of interpersonal relationships, company productivity, and customer service.

Linda is the executive director of a nonprofit center providing mental health services for veterans in a large community. She and her staff have been very busy over the past week preparing for the end-of-year board meeting to review goals and strategies for the coming year. As she is reviewing her notes, one of the more vocal and influential members of the board, Robert, sticks his head in the door.

"Hi, Linda," he says cheerily. "Mind if I have a quick word with you?"

"Sure, what's up?" she replies, motioning him to a seat.

"Well, as you know, we will be reviewing what you have planned for the coming year at this week's board meeting. I believe, and I think you will agree, that it is vital that we broaden our services to include providing mental health services to homeless families." He pauses and looks at Linda. "You do think this is an important service, don't you?"

"That is certainly one of the services we should be considering," replies Linda.

"Then let me get straight to the point. Margaret Morris, the board co-chair, and I disagree on this topic. I am convinced that expanding our services to homeless families is the right thing to do, and Margaret is just being stubborn about this opportunity. I think it is important that you take a strong stand in the board meeting so that she will rethink her position. Can I count on you to back me up?"

This scenario illustrates an important dynamic that occurs between individuals in healthcare organizations, business, not-for-profits, universities, government agencies, and associations on a daily basis. Subordinates, coworkers, and managers often approach someone else with their view of a problem and try to enlist the other individual as a supporter.

In this case, Robert has a conflict with a fellow board member, and is consciously or unconsciously trying to co-opt Linda by convincing her to "take his side." Given her position as executive director, it would not be prudent for Linda to join the conflict between Robert and Margaret. First, this is a no-win situation. If Linda agrees to support Robert, she could very easily alienate Margaret. If, on the other hand, she supports Margaret, she could alienate Robert. Second, Linda does not really understand why Robert and Margaret feel the way they do. Referring back to the CCGA process model, Linda only understands that a conflict exists, and Robert's goal—that he wants to expand services to the homeless. Third, taking sides or trying to solve the conflict herself will not help Robert or Margaret work more effectively through this and future problems themselves.

One of Linda's roles as the executive director is to foster board development. This means helping board members work well with each other. Conflicts and opportunities to improve are routine occurrences of any organization. Simply put, Margaret and Robert are adults and are fully capable of resolving this conflict themselves. Linda can play an effective role as a coach to help Margaret and Robert address the conflict together.

In chapter one you learned that a major reason healthcare organizations fail to resolve conflict effectively is that managers and employees do not share, practice, and hold each other accountable to appropriate standards of behavior and conduct. The CCGA mediation process provides both managers and employees with a logical method for helping each other consider the viewpoints of others, address conflict at the lowest possible level, and apply the conflict-mediation and communication skills learned.

CONFLICT and COACHING

Take a minute to look at the CCGA mediation model below (Figure 13). Notice that the model and sequence are exactly the same, but the questions suggested for each step have changed to reflect a coaching point of view.

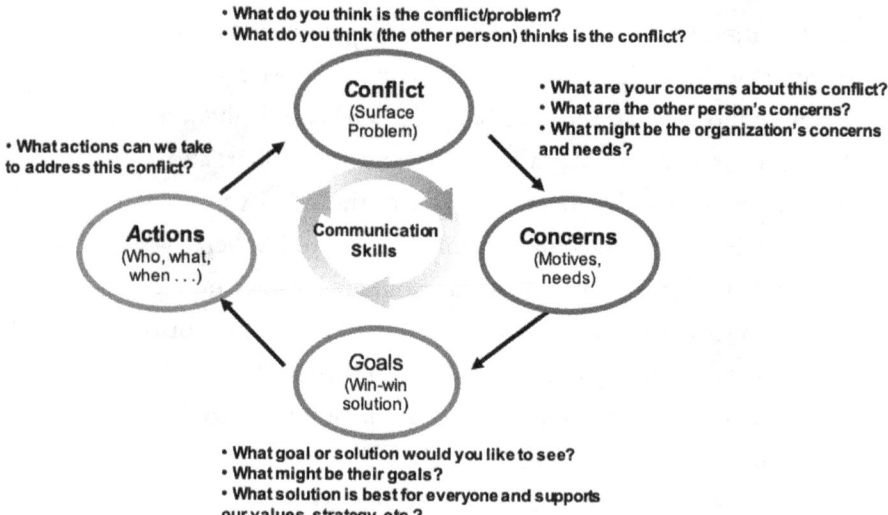

Figure 13: Coaching Others in Conflict Diagram

A key benefit of the CCGA mediation process model is to provide managers and employees with a simple process for solving problems with others and an effective method of coaching others in conflict. This is important because the sooner we can resolve a conflict, the less time that conflict will have to grow and degrade relationships, patient care, customer service, and productivity. We have found that at home and in the workplace, most conflicts can be addressed by the people most closely involved. Because conflict is not always a positive experience, we often see individuals attempt either to build alliances or gain support from others, or influence someone in a decision-making position to solve the conflict in their favor. The problem with these approaches is that by attempting to build alliances, we often simply create silos or cliques of distrust. It becomes "us" against "them." In addition, if we constantly look for someone else to solve conflicts, we fail to take personal responsibility and accountability for acting in ways that would build trust and resolve conflicts quickly.

For example, let's assume that in the previous case, Linda, the nonprofit staff, and the board members have been trained in the conflict-mediation process and effective communication skills. During that training, they would have reviewed or developed principles that outline their values, roles, and guidelines for behavior. Let's see how Linda might respond in such a manner as to be respectful to both Robert and Margaret, while not taking responsibility for "solving" the conflict, using the framework suggested at the beginning of this chapter. As you read the narrative below, try and see if you can identify how Linda is using the CCGA mediation process model to coach Robert to address the conflict directly with Margaret.

"Let me make sure I understand what you're saying, Robert," replies Linda. "You feel that it is important that we broaden our mental health services to include homeless families. Is that right?"

"That is exactly what I am saying," Robert responds.

Linda continues, "And Margaret does not share your view on this issue?"

"No, as I said, she is being obstinate and just can't seem to see why this would be valuable to our organization," says Robert.

"So, the problem or conflict seems to be that you and Margaret disagree on the issue of whether to serve homeless families in the coming year. Is that correct?" states Linda.

Robert leans forward. "Linda, that's what I am saying. Now, I need you to straighten Margaret out once and for all so we can get this issue behind us and work on other important goals."

"Robert," Linda says, "have you asked Margaret how she sees this issue? Do you know what her concerns are, or have you explained yours to her?"

"Well," Robert says slowly, "no, I haven't had the chance. But it's no use. She has already made up her mind."

"Even if she has made up her mind, shouldn't you two be working together and with the rest of the board to share what you hope to see in the coming year, why you feel the way you do, key goals, and what actions and resources you think are necessary?" says Linda. "Let me suggest this—suppose you set up a time to meet with Margaret to talk about this issue?"

Robert shifts in his seat, saying, "I guess I could, but I am not sure what I would say."

Linda responds, "If you think she will be resistant, what could you say that might help get the discussion started?"

Robert says, "I guess I could see if she sees the opportunity like I do, and ask her why she feels her view is so important."

"That sounds reasonable. What can you do next?" Linda inquires.

Robert smiles. "Okay, okay, I see what you are doing. I remember the training. I can share my concerns, make sure I understand hers, and then see what each other's goals are and consider any actions we might take."

"Great," Linda replies. "That sounds like a good plan. Please touch base with me and let me know how it went."

What happened during this interchange between Linda and Robert? First, she did not respond to Robert's immediate request that she support him by taking sides against Margaret. Rather, she made sure she understood the problem as identified by Robert. (Margaret was not there, so Linda did not attempt to suggest she understood how Margaret saw the conflict.) Once Robert confirmed that Linda understood the conflict from his point of view, Linda asked if he understood how Margaret saw the problem, and what her concerns might be. When Robert said he had not talked with Margaret on this issue, Linda suggested he do so. Note that she did not offer to be there too. While it might be necessary in some cases, remember the goal of the conflict-mediation system is for competent, capable individuals to resolve conflicts themselves. It is also important to note that Linda has modeled effective communication skills. She clarified Robert's view of the situation, paraphrased frequently to ensure understanding, and acknowledged his feelings.

FOLLOW-UP COACHING

Suppose that Robert says he feels uncomfortable meeting with Margaret, or continues to maintain, "I don't know what to say to her." Linda can continue to use the same CCGA mediation process to model and role-play how Robert's interaction with Margaret might be enacted. For example:

Robert leans back in his chair and sighs, "Linda, that sounds great, but I really don't know what Margaret and I would have to talk about. Can't you just deal with this conflict for us?"

"I suppose I could," replies Linda. "But I think this is something that you two can and should work out yourselves. After all, I suspect other conflicts or opportunities to consider new programs or services will certainly occur in the future—won't they?"

"Yeah, I suppose so," Robert concedes.

"Okay," says Linda. "How could you find out how she sees this issue?"

"I guess I could ask her what her concerns are regarding homeless families and their mental health issues," Robert says.

Linda persists. "That sounds reasonable. What would you say next?"

"I could tell her why I think the mental health issues of homeless families are a problem and explain my concerns," Robert suggests. "But what if she just disagrees with me? Aren't we just right back to square one?"

"Good point. If she sees the problem differently from you, she probably will disagree," Linda agrees. "But what are you going to do if and when that happens? Isn't it important that you two work through this together?"

"Yeah," he says.

"I would recommend that when you meet, you diagram the CCGA process on a piece of paper or the whiteboard like we learned. You know—what is the conflict from your point of view? What is the conflict from her point of view? What are your concerns and what are hers?" Linda suggests.

"You mean lay my cards on the table, just like that?" Robert says, raising his eyebrows.

"Yes. What would be the benefit?" Linda asks.

"Well, Margaret would not think I was trying to hide anything. But this sounds so simplistic. I can't believe it will solve our conflict," says Robert.

"You're right. It may not resolve the entire issue, but what will it do for both of you and the organization?" Linda responds.

Robert stands. "It will help us understand where each other are coming from and why."

"Right!" replies Linda. "I'd actually like to hear how the conversation goes. Can you follow up and let me know what happens after you talk with Margaret? Would you like to use my phone to call and see if you can set up the meeting?"

As in the first interchange, Linda has employed effective listening skills and avoided taking on the responsibility of "solving" the conflict between Robert and Margaret. Instead, she has coached him through his own doubts and helped him consider how he can approach Margaret by mapping out the CCGA process from his viewpoint and sharing it with Margaret. Linda also reminded Robert of the importance of him and Margaret working together as board members. Finally, Linda has pressed him to take action by asking when he would contact Margaret.

Note that Linda also observed that she would like Robert to follow up with her. This is a key step that managers, supervisors, and team leaders should consider. In many cases, it may not be necessary for two individuals in conflict to check back with you. In other situations, it may be important that you *require* the individuals to report back. This "closes the loop," and ensures you stay informed regarding how effectively the conflict was addressed and the status of the relationship between these two individuals. Moreover, if additional coaching is needed, you can provide it at that time.

GROUP COACHING

When individuals are skilled in the conflict-mediation process, they are in a position to resolve most routine conflicts that arise. Sometimes, conflicts may occur that require an objective perspective. A group coach may be needed when one or more of the parties has become so emotionally engaged that they cannot separate themselves from the problem or solution. Disagreements or misunderstandings may grow to a point that the conflict threatens unity or relationships with others. If the conflict is not surfaced and resolved, individuals may let the problem fester. As a result, stress, tension, and bad feelings may hinder productivity and eat away at morale.

Another occasion in which a group coach might be needed is when an individual or group faces a problem that is beyond their scope of responsibility, knowledge, or resources. All individuals, teams, and managers have limits or boundaries on knowledge, skills, roles, responsibilities, budgets, time, and so on. When limits such as these are reached, it is often necessary to request assistance or guidance from others or one's management.

Use of a group coach should not be looked on as a failure by the participants. As suggested above, there are legitimate reasons for relying on a group coach. The important thing to remember is to assess each opportunity and determine if the conflict is one which could be reasonably resolved by those closely involved. If so, coach the individuals through the CCGA mediation process. If you determine that the problem, if not resolved quickly, will impact relationships, productivity, service, or efficiency, then you may want to serve as or appoint a group-conflict coach.

There are two common methods of group-conflict coaching. First, you might ask or appoint a team member or other third party to serve as the group-conflict coach. This individual should understand the standards of conduct and behavior, be skilled in the CCGA mediation process, and be a good communicator. The second method of group-conflict coaching is for the manager or team leader to serve in this role.

Group-Conflict Coaching Example

Thus far we have seen how Linda might coach Robert and Margaret to attempt to resolve the conflict on their own. Suppose that Robert and Margaret try to resolve the conflict but are unable to do so. Take a look at the following interchange:

Linda is standing at her whiteboard diagramming her board presentation when she hears a knock. She turns to see both Margaret and Robert standing at the door.

"Sorry to interrupt, Linda," Margaret says, "but Robert and I are stuck on a major issue and need your help. Do you have a minute?"

"Sure, I am just finishing up," Linda observes. "I have about ten minutes before my staff meeting. What can I do?"

"Well," Robert says, "as you and I discussed, I arranged a meeting with Margaret to discuss our views on the issue of mental health services for homeless families. However—"

"What Robert is trying to say," Margaret interjects, "is that we can't seem to get anywhere with each other. Robert just can't seem to understand why focusing on the homeless is out of the question."

"Robert, Margaret," Linda responds, "I am more than willing to help you discuss this issue. What would you like for me to do?"

"Help us work through this conflict!" responds Robert.

"Okay, but understand that we are going to use the conflict-mediation system we learned about at our board retreat last year. Just to remind you, we agreed to communicate in ways that advance our values, build relationships, and create trust. Remember?" Linda inquires.

"Sure, that was a good retreat," says Margaret.

Linda walks to a clear part of the whiteboard and draws the CCGA mediation process. "Do you two remember what this stands for?"

"Yes," says Robert. "The *C*s stands for conflict and concerns, *G* is for Goals, and *A* is for actions."

"Good," says Linda. "When Robert and I talked earlier, it appeared that the conflict was that you two disagree regarding whether mental health services for homeless families should be a major focus for the coming year. Is that right?"

Both Margaret and Robert nod.

"So, I will write that down as the conflict. Now, Robert, what are your concerns about serving homeless families?" Linda asks.

Robert shrugs. "There are a couple of needs. First, with the downturn in the economy, the unemployment rate has risen by a little over 4 percent. Many of those who have lost their jobs are losing their homes because they can't afford the house payments. While most will find jobs eventually, they still experience significant stress, depression, and anxiety over the challenges they face. This includes the pressures felt by all members of the families—children included."

"Thanks, Robert," Linda says as she writes Robert's concerns on the CCGA diagram. "What are your concerns regarding the homeless, Margaret?"

"Well, first I would agree that the economy has been bad and unemployment is way up," Margaret shares. "But I think our most important priority should be focusing our resources on veterans and perhaps expanding so that we also provide veterans with additional job skills so they get new, better jobs."

"So, your concern is that our resources should be focused entirely on veterans; is that right?" Linda summarizes.

"Yes." Margaret nods.

"See?" asks Robert. "There is no way to close the gap between what Margaret thinks is the right thing to do and what I think we should do."

"Well, when I look at the concerns you two have listed, and consider the values and goals of the organization, I see some overlap. Both of you want to offer support to people who need mental health services—is that correct?" Linda suggests.

"Yes, I guess you could say that," Robert says.

"I wonder if there is a way of providing mental health services to veterans and to homeless families at the same time?" Linda observes.

"I have not really considered that, and I can't see how we would find the resources, but I suppose it's possible," says Margaret.

Robert nods thoughtfully. "I have not considered that either, and I can see Margaret's point about wanting to focus our resources. Perhaps we could serve the mental health issues for homeless veterans and their family members too."

"Well, that would keep our resources focused on our primary client group. I can see where helping family members also helps the vets too," replies Margaret.

"Good point," notes Linda. "Listen, I need to go to my staff meeting. So far we have your view of the conflict and concerns identified. Suppose I leave you two here with the whiteboard to begin working on goals and actions? I'll come back after the staff meeting."

"Sure," says Robert. "But I am not saying this issue is resolved. I am just saying there may be some overlap."

"Neither am I," says Margaret.

"I understand. You two get as far as you can, and I will check back in an hour," says Linda as she picks up her staff-meeting notes and heads for the door.

In this example, Linda took a more active role as a conflict coach. Margaret and Robert began with some snide remarks, so Linda tactfully reminded them of their earlier retreat and agreement to communicate in a respectful manner. Linda then had each reiterate how they saw the conflict, and their concerns. Note that Linda was careful to write these responses on the whiteboard where all could see. Linda could easily have used a piece of paper or a page on a flipchart as well. In addition to making Margaret and Robert's thinking explicit, diagramming the conflict visually ensured that all relevant data was captured. Linda, Margaret, and Robert know who said what, and why they feel the way they do. In a sense, putting the "conflict" on a whiteboard, flipchart page, or piece of paper objectifies the problem or opportunity so people can focus on the issue and not each other.

Also, remember that Linda's goal is to coach Margaret and Robert to resolve as much of this conflict as possible on their own. In this scenario, once the two board members reached some agreement and momentum regarding how their concerns might overlap, Linda took the opportunity to return the process back to them to work on together. Certainly, Linda could have stayed and helped them work through the entire CCGA process. However, since both Margaret and Robert are skilled communicators, and have reached some level of understanding of each other's concerns, it does not hurt to let them continue alone. Linda did make a point of saying she would return after the staff meeting to see how they were doing. If they are still stuck, Linda could continue to coach as needed.

While Linda happens to be the executive director of the nonprofit organization, the coaching skills she demonstrated in this case could be applied by anyone in the organization at any level. An employee could have coached Linda through a conflict with a board member or funding source. One employee could coach another employee who is having a conflict with a client or volunteer. In short, the conflict-mediation system can be applied effectively by anyone, anytime.

In the next chapter, you will learn how to design and implement a conflict-mediation system within your healthcare organization.

The Least You Need to Remember

➢ The CCGA process is an effective tool for coaching others through conflict.

➢ An individual may coach another peer, employee, or in a group setting.

➢ Coaching ensures that others learn and practice the skills they need to resolve conflict at the lowest possible level.

➢ When coaching an employee through a situation of conflict, the manager may want to follow up with the individual to ensure the conflict is adequately addressed or determine if additional support is needed.

CHAPTER 5 TOOLS and ACTIVITIES

Personal-Coaching Map

Think about some of the relationships you have with subordinates, peers, or management. Is there a conflict, problem, or misunderstanding occurring between two or more individuals, or two or more groups, that could benefit from coaching? A blank CCGA template is provided below. Take a few minutes to diagram how you might coach each person through the conflict in order to achieve a more effective resolution.

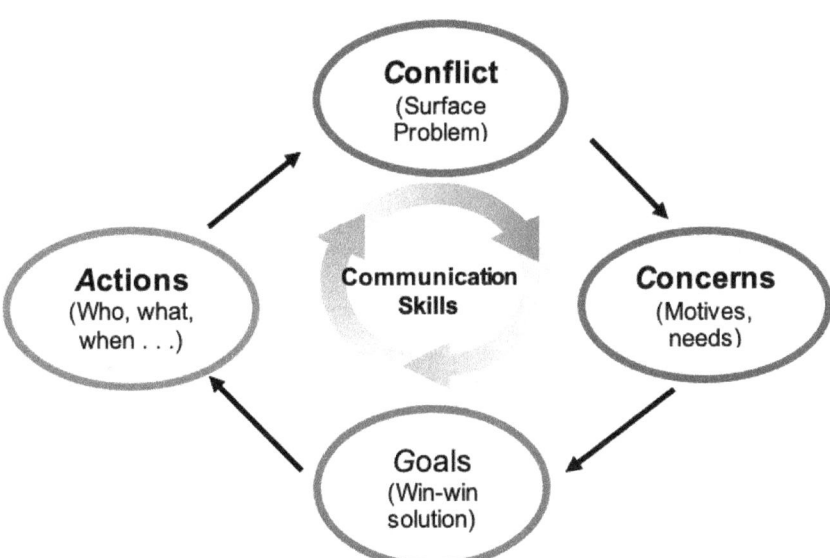

Chapter 6

IMPLEMENTING THE CONFLICT-MEDIATION SYSTEM

> *When we quit thinking primarily about*
> *ourselves and our own self-preservation, we*
> *undergo a truly heroic transformation of consciousness.*
> —Joseph Campbell

In This Chapter

In this chapter, you will learn how to implement the conflict-mediation system within your organization or area of influence within the organization. You will learn that the conflict-mediation system can be customized to any healthcare organization. When creating training for your healthcare organization, you can create examples and case studies that accurately mirror the type of conflicts or challenges your management, employees, patients, and customers face on a routine basis. You will also learn a proven, systematic approach for ensuring that key stakeholders are involved in conceptualizing, developing, implementing, and improving the conflict-mediation system in your healthcare organization.

How can you decide if implementing the conflict-mediation system is appropriate for your healthcare organization? We recommend that you start by determining to what extent unproductive conflict is eating away at employee morale, customer service, patient care, and overall organizational effectiveness. There are numerous methods for getting an idea of the extent of the impact unproductive conflict might be having on your healthcare organization:

- When you look at your customer surveys, is patient care or customer service suffering due to lack of teamwork or poor communication?
- Do employee-satisfaction surveys suggest that morale is poor?
- Do employee surveys suggest that managers and supervisors lack the skills and resolve to deal effectively with conflict?
- Is there an increase in violations or "close calls" in adhering to values, ethics, or codes of conduct?
- Are grievances or safety violations occurring more frequently than desired?
- Do management and employees frequently "look the other way" or avoid confrontation instead of addressing unproductive conflict?
- When conflicts or disagreements occur, do they escalate beyond what is reasonable?
- Are you seeing an increase in sick days or employee turnover?
- Do you feel like there is a climate of "us versus them" in your organization?

If these and/or other measures suggest that unproductive conflict is obstructing success, you had better do *something*! Otherwise, you are modeling the definition of insanity—doing the same thing repeatedly, but expecting a different result.

Healthcare organizations interested in integrating the conflict-mediation system into their culture and training programs often have two concerns. First, they want to understand how compatible the system is with existing organizational culture, values, and training. Fortunately, the conflict-mediation system is designed to be easily integrated into any existing training programs or serve as a stand-alone workshop.

The training consists of
1. learning and practicing the CCGA process with case studies and actual problems, opportunities, and conflicts from your work setting,
2. learning and practicing the CLARC communication skills, and if desired,
3. teaching an additional workshop on conflict coaching skills for all employees, interested employees, or individuals identified as excellent coaches (team or unit leaders, managers and supervisor, human resources personnel, etc.).

In addition, as you learned in chapter two, this system should be based on your company values and standards of conduct and behavior.

Second, managers or department heads are often interested to learn if they can implement this system within their unit or area of influence rather than throughout the healthcare organization. The conflict-mediation system is easily scalable for an entire healthcare organization or unit or team level within that organization. In fact, some healthcare organizations prefer to "test" the system out on a small scale before implementing on a broader scale. In other cases, a manager, director, or vice president may simply desire to have the process implemented within their area of responsibility.

This chapter will describe how your healthcare organization can customize and implement the conflict-mediation process in a thoughtful manner that achieves significant results, enhances morale, builds trust, and promotes better patient care and/or customer service.

WHY CUSTOMIZE?

Every healthcare organization and most units within the organization feel they are different and unique. Culture, service processes, functional responsibilities, skill sets, and other factors may influence how an organization or unit decides to develop and implement change. How the conflict-mediation system is implemented within an organization may take various forms. You can implement the process company-wide, by functional division, geographical locales, at the department level, or for a specific group of individuals such as management. Any approach can be effective. The key is to develop and implement the system in a way that is well considered, well communicated, and aligned with organizational strategy and goals.

CUSTOMIZATION PROCESS

The suggested process for customizing and implementing this process in an organization is illustrated in Figure 14. Each of the steps will be described in more detail in this chapter.

Step One:	Form a Steering Team
Step Two:	Determine Standards
Step Three:	Identify Training Needs
Step Four:	Develop Roll-out Plan
Step Five:	Pilot and Improve Training
Step Six:	Implement
Step Seven:	Evaluate, Communicate Results, and Improve

Figure 14: Customization Process

There are several reasons most healthcare organizations do not respond successfully to everyday conflict. First, many managers and employees have not had any training in conflict-management skills. Second, many organizations rely on human resources or external mediators to help disputing parties to resolve conflict. While it may be appropriate to have referees on the field during a football or baseball game to resolve conflicts, or to have professional mediators for some employee or organizational disputes, it is not very practical or cost effective to rely on professional mediators for the vast majority of conflicts that take place in the workplace. Similarly, if you need to stop and run to human resources every time a conflict occurs, you are wasting time. Moreover, if you think about it, if a problem or conflict is so big that you need to bring in a professional mediator or get human resources involved, it has probably been going on for some time, and the damage to relationships, quality, productivity, and perhaps even patient care and/or customer service is already substantial.

Third, few people actually apply the skills they learn in most conflict-management training programs. How many times have you attended a workshop you thought was excellent, only to go back to a work environment that did not support the new skills you learned? Unlike other conflict-management training programs, the conflict-mediation system is also a culture-change effort. The expressed intention of this process is to establish a culture and environment where managers and employees embrace and *apply* the skills of conflict mediation themselves on a daily basis and thereby reinforce the organization's culture. This process and the skills learned give everyone a common language and approach for looking at and addressing changes, opportunities, challenges, and conflict at the lowest possible level.

For this reason, it is recommended that a team of individuals be tasked with planning how the steps for implementing and sustaining the process company-wide should be carried out and by whom. Tasking a team with the responsibility of implementing this process suggests that there should be someone who acts as the sponsor of this effort. This individual may be the CEO, another executive, or someone else with the authority to provide the team with the resources and support it needs to succeed.

Step One: Create a Steering Team

In small healthcare organizations, the steering team may be composed of only two or three individuals who are responsible for arranging for training, communication, aligning the culture of the organization with the values of the conflict-mediation initiative, establishing metrics to measure progress, and establishing incentives for positive behavior (see Figure 15).

Figure 15: Small Steering Team

In large healthcare organizations, we recommend selecting representatives from several areas, such as professional specialties (doctors, nurses, lab technicians, etc.), marketing, human resources, finance, information technology, laboratories, volunteers, the legal department, suppliers, and even patient representatives. If your healthcare organization has multiple locations, you may want a primary steering team with other sub-teams providing input from the different sites or even different countries if necessary (see Figure 16). The important point is that those individuals who are responsible for ensuring the implementation within your organization be seen as credible and capable of seeing the project through to completion and that everyone feels they have had input into the design.

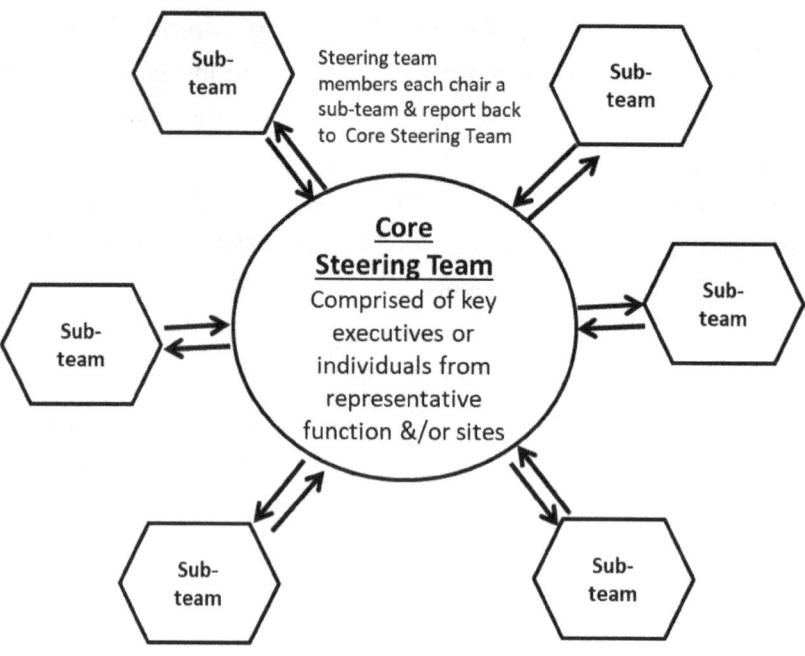

Figure 16: Large-Organization Design Team

Step Two: Create an Inspirational Culture

Once the steering and/or sub-team(s) has been convened, their first task should be to determine what culture the organization should have in order to bring out the best in everyone. Simply defined, culture is "the written and unwritten rules by which people get their work done"—the everyday reality of organizational life. Culture is *not* the organization's vision, mission statement, the employee handbook, or the posters you have on your walls. Culture is what you do, how you do it, how you behave, how you communicate, and how you treat each other, your customers, and yourself. Speeches, grand plans, videos, brochures, training manuals, and T-shirts that promote a lofty institutional purpose all have some influence on culture, but if these do not align with how people *really* behave, then the negative impact can be substantial.

Let us explain why this is so important. As you can see in Figure

17 below, there are two options for implementing any change plan. One option is to have a clear idea of your institutional purpose and desired outcomes, and to clarify, implement, and sustain an inspirational culture designed to encourage and support constant movement toward that purpose and those goals. The other option is to state a lofty institutional purpose and goals, and then maintain your current culture as is.

If you are struggling now, then your current culture is maintaining the status quo. If you do not change the culture to encourage and support growth toward the desired institutional purpose and goals, then you will find, as Peter Drucker so aptly observed, "culture eats strategy for breakfast." In simple terms, nothing will change. Worse, by touting a lofty purpose and goals without changing the culture as needed to succeed, you simply demotivate people, and performance can quickly go downhill. Moreover, you are potentially competing against other institutions that are doing what they need to do to improve, so even if you maintain your status quo, you are declining compared to your competition. Generally, this is not a recipe for career or organizational success.

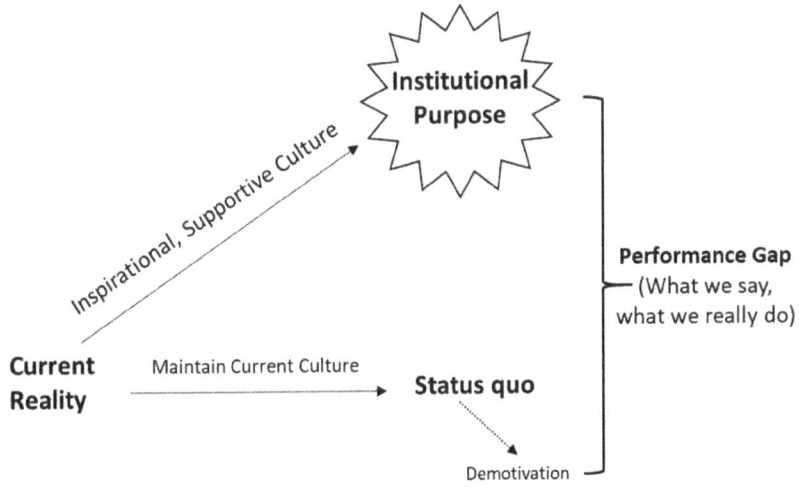

Figure 17: Culture and Change

How do you avoid this dilemma? There are two ways of building an organizational culture. One way is to do so with thoughtful consideration and conscious intent. The other way is to let the culture evolve on its own with little thought put into the process. Following are some suggestions for taking the thoughtful, conscious approach.

Conduct Representative Focus Groups

Determine what is and is not working at your healthcare institution given the purpose and outcomes desired.

- What is the current culture?
- What actions, behaviors, or artifacts illustrate the current culture?
- What would the ideal culture look like? Why?
- What actions, behaviors, or artifacts would illustrate the desired culture?
- What difference would these improvements make?
- What do you need to start doing and stop doing to see improvement? (Changes in policies, procedures, training, behavior, etc.)
- How will you measure and recognize positive individual, group, and organizational progress?
- What will you do about those who do not buy into this effort?

Establish Operating Values

Recall that values tell us what to do and what not to do. Values become the standards of our actions and behaviors, guide how we treat other people, and ultimately influence the culture of the organization. If the organization does not already have a well-defined and accepted set of values, you need to develop values that all employees or members can support. If the organizational values are truly "lived" in your daily interactions, then the culture will be strong, and greater trust will result. If the values are stated but only given lip service, then the culture will be weak, trust will be limited, and the ability to resolve conflict will be significantly impaired.

Developing values is not a quick or easy process. The team should consider a number of questions when determining their values:
- What do we stand for?
- What behaviors would illustrate what we stand for?
- How do we want to treat each other, our customers, and our suppliers?
- How do we want to be viewed by the community and our customers?
- What attitudes and behaviors do we want to recognize and reward?

The answers to these questions should lead the team to identify a number of key values. This list of values will probably be different for every organization. The team can then define the values and share them with focus groups of other employees to obtain their review and suggestions for improvement. Once the list is complete, it should be communicated widely along with examples of behaviors that exemplify each value.

Create a Safe Environment

High-performing healthcare organizations create an environment where members are skilled at communicating each other's thoughts, ideas, and conflicts without resorting to ridicule, threats, or passive-aggressive competition. This level of high-performing work environment is developed by valuing confidentiality, establishing a conflict-mediation system, and using communication that does not naturally seek to place blame or guilt on others for conflicts and disputes. The design team should take a critical look at the behaviors and practices that currently exist within the organization and detract from a safe environment.

For example, we were asked to conduct the conflict-to-cooperation workshop for an international manufacturer of electronic components. At the "kickoff session," the vice president for operations stalked angrily to the front of the class and snarled, "You people better listen up and learn this information! I am sick and tired of all the conflict that takes place here! You better get it right—or else!" Then he stormed out of the room. We learned later that he was perceived as a very angry, abrasive individual known for "taking names and kicking butt." As you might imagine, his behavior and management approach contributed to an environment where people did not feel safe and certainly did not contribute to an environment where those attending the training eagerly transferred their new skills back to the job!

Collaborative Communication Skills

Effective communication is very important for effective work between the executives, management, employees, patients, customers, and suppliers. While many of us have received training in public speaking, few of us have received training in listening skills. Effective communication is both speaking *and* listening. Your healthcare organization may need to implement training opportunities for individual members that provide them with the skills they need to present their ideas and suggestions effectively and then listen appropriately to others. The CLARC skills (Confront, Listen, Acknowledge, Respond, and Commit) are based on effective listening and speaking skills and can serve as an effective basis from which to design and/or implement your communication-skills training programs.

Power Management

As described in chapter two, there are very real differences in power between people in organizations. Executives, management, and other employees must recognize, acknowledge, and apply their differences in status, authority, responsibility, expertise, competency, and personality to enhance organizational improvement and patient/

customer care. In so doing, organizations and the individuals within those organizations feel empowered to share the full extent of their knowledge and skills to resolve problems.

How power is managed within an organization is a clear reflection of its culture. This means the design team must pay close attention to understanding how decisions get made, who makes them, and why. They can then consider if the existing power-management structure is appropriate or if changes need to be made in policies or procedures that reward different behaviors.

Some organizations choose to identify individuals to serve as process facilitators for meetings that involve discussions about conflicts, problems, opportunities, or other changes. A process facilitator is trained to facilitate the discussion, clarify communication, prevent miscommunication, and assist the group in the application of appropriate problem-solving and decision-making methods.

Step Three: Identify Training Needs

Training in conflict mediation and communication skills should be provided to the following groups:

1. All Employees: Because this is an effort to build conflict management into the entire culture of the healthcare organization, all new and current employees, staff, managers, and executives should receive the basic training. We have found that the CCGA process and communication skills can be learned within a day or two.

It is also suggested that an organization develop case examples that are realistic and applicable to the types of conflicts routinely experienced by employees at all levels of the organization. These case examples should be designed to illustrate "real-life" examples of productive and unproductive situations of conflict for specific groups, such as nursing staff, laboratory, doctors, pharmacy, marketing, finance, human resources, patients and families, volunteers, suppliers, regulators, etc. Providing practical job-related case examples with which participants can readily identify adds realism, familiarity, and helps ensure rapid transfer of these skills to the job. Some organizations add an additional benefit to their training by including opportunities for employees to practice the CCGA model in family and other social or community situations.

2. Managers, Team Leaders, and Facilitators: After attending basic conflict training, managers, team leaders, and others identified as conflict-mediation facilitators should attend training to enhance their skills to coach others. This training should provide a clear understanding of how to coach individuals or small groups to resolve conflicts themselves; serve as facilitators in routine meetings, small and large group situations; and serve as exceptional models of the CLARC communication skills. It is not uncommon for these individuals to be asked to conduct all or at least some portions of the basic all-employee training. Having internal experts teach these courses helps other employees see them as "go-to" experts when difficult issues or conflicts arise.

This level of training can typically be learned by participants within a day. As with the initial training described above, it is suggested that this workshop also include practical examples of opportunities for managers, team leaders, and facilitators to coach others on the job.

Note: It is recommended that individuals who will conduct basic or advanced training in the CCGA process and communication/facilitation skills attend some type of "train-the-trainer" workshop. The authors can provide trained facilitators to conduct this training or can train your internal facilitators to conduct the training themselves. This "train-the-trainer" workshop exposes your facilitators to the conflict training and support materials, and allows them to co-facilitate with our skilled trainers so they are comfortable and well trained to conduct the training from that point forward.

In the process of planning the principles for implementing the conflict-mediation process, the design team may also identify additional skills and knowledge that are necessary for the process to be more effective within that organization and culture. These could include presentation skills, meeting management, problem-solving, sensitivity to culture and diversity issues, coaching, and team building.

If the healthcare organization has skilled curriculum-design staff who can integrate these programs into the organization's culture, training can be developed in-house and some may be provided online. Other organizations find it is easier to have their in-house trainers certified to teach this content and simply purchase the training materials for one or both programs. These training materials may be obtained in a generic format or customized specifically for the organization and conducted with trained professionals.

As suggested above, many healthcare organizations find it is best to have one or more of their internal instructors co-facilitate with an external trainer. The value of this approach is that the external trainer brings deep knowledge and experience in conflict mediation and can share perspectives from many different organizations and workgroups. The internal facilitator can provide clear guidance to how the process is applied and sustained within the organization, as well as help participants see the practical application of the training on-the-job.

Step Four: Develop Implementation Plan

Great training and an effective operating framework do not mean you will have limitless success. There also needs to be a plan for implementing the conflict-mediation process. Considerations may include the following:

- How will the effort be communicated ahead of time?
- Which groups will be trained first? Which will be trained second?
- How many training sessions will be needed?
- When and where will the training be held?
- Who will provide the training?

- What support materials will participants receive during training?
- What support will units receive from coaches or facilitators over time?
- What policies, procedures, or other organizational systems or processes must be modified, eliminated, or developed to sustain the effort?
- How will new employees be oriented to this process?

Step Five: Pilot and Improve Training

For medium and large healthcare organizations, it may be prudent to test or "pilot" the training program on a sample group of executives, managers, and/or employees. The purpose of the pilot training is to obtain reactions, identify areas for improving the curriculum, facilitation, logistics, and communications, and build support needed to sustain the training on the job.

Once the pilot or test training programs are complete, the design team should oversee any improvements needed to ensure the knowledge and skills learned are easily and effectively transmitted to future participants. Changes to the cases used, location of the training programs, way the material is facilitated, and program length may also be needed.

If the design team has determined that it is best to have internal staff conduct or co-facilitate the training programs, these individuals need to be trained. Most often, train-the-trainer programs begin with the individual first attending the basic training as a participant. After attending as a participant, the individual may observe a workshop to take notes, or, if they are skilled enough, simply co-facilitate a workshop with a skilled presenter. The final step is to take the lead role as workshop trainer with a skilled presenter as backup.

Step Six: Implement

After any needed improvements to the curriculum, audiovisual aids, and training methods, it is time to implement the training. We recommend that organizations take a top-down approach, meaning that executives and managers attend the basic and higher-level training first or at least attend the training with their subordinates. The advantage of this approach is that these individuals have a great deal of influence on how successfully the effort is perceived and applied in the workplace. By attending the training first or attending with everyone else, they are able to describe and communicate not only the purpose of the training but also its integration with the healthcare organization's culture. Further, the executives and managers should be models of effective implementation!

Step Seven: Plan for the Future

It is also important to consider future employees. Any organization continually adds new employees. Some consideration should be given to ensure that all new employees are oriented to the conflict-mediation system in new-employee orientation and through new-employee or new-manager training. How will those being recruited be informed of the institution's purpose, desired outcomes, and culture before they are hired so they clearly understand what is expected? Once a new person is hired and begins their orientation to the institution, what training and mentoring will they receive so that they clearly understand what is expected behavior, what they cannot do, how they should communicate, and what they should do if they are bullied, harassed, discriminated against, or experience some other form of disrespectful or uncivil behavior?

Step Eight: Monitor and Communicate Results

Providing employee and manager training is not the final step. It is important for the design team to follow up and monitor the training process, review participant evaluations, measure actual improvements in the workplace (morale, turnover, grievances, etc.), and recommend additional improvements. As the organization and participants gain experience, they will almost certainly discover ways of continually adapting training to reflect new conflicts, challenges, and opportunities. These changes may include new and better ways of teaching the workshop content, incorporating more relevant case studies or examples, and requiring new-employee groups or divisions to attend the training. Facilitators and management will also learn better ways of implementing and coaching others on the job. By monitoring both the training and its transfer to the workplace, the design team can ensure that the curriculum is constantly updated and refreshed to drive increased application and productivity.

The purpose of the conflict-mediation process is to significantly enhance organizational and employee productivity, morale, profitability, and/or levels of patient customer service. In the process of mapping out the operating framework, the design team should have identified what kinds of outcomes to expect:

- In the months following the training, have the number of reported conflicts decreased?
- Has employee and manager retention improved?
- Are employees reporting higher levels of morale and confidence in voicing their opinion?
- Have you noticed on your customer surveys that service levels or patient quality improved?
- Have errors decreased?
- Has customer satisfaction increased?
- Are there other measures that would be important to your organization that you should track and report?

It is important to identify the bottom line and human impact your organization would like to see achieved when implementing this program.

A major factor in the ongoing success of this process is to communicate successes to all employees and reward the individuals or groups who were responsible. Communication channels may include newsletters, staff meetings, special-recognition events, emails, and bulletin boards. The important point is that the communication should be clear, frequent, and should describe how the ability to mediate conflicts effectively has improved morale, interpersonal relationships, retention, and productivity.

CASE EXAMPLE #3: ANGELS of MERCY

Let's look at a hospital system that decided to implement the conflict-mediation system within their culture. Angels of Mercy was a church-owned hospital with 250 beds. Their reputation in town was good, although they were not considered to be the "go-to" facility for the best care. In 2010, the entire healthcare industry began to make adjustments to comply with the Affordable Care Act. After becoming familiar with the provisions of the Affordable Care Act, Angels of Mercy did not think they would see any major change in the services provided or patient mix as they had already been admitting their share of Medicaid patients. However, in 2013 they completed their Community Health Assessment identifying key community health needs and issues through a systematic, comprehensive data-collection process. Based on the results of this assessment, Angels of Mercy developed a more accurate picture of the health needs of its community.

After reviewing the assessment results, senior management concluded that Angels of Mercy needed to improve services to the community in three areas: access to emergency care, better information for patients with diabetes, and better preventative information and treatment for obesity. Those changes were going to challenge the hospital to inform the community of these three services, provide better information to individuals who might need the services, and to provide different care or treatment and more frequently.

It became clear to the executive team that a new strategy was needed to implement the changes. In response, the executive team tasked their administrative services director (ASD) with developing and implementing a new strategy based on informing the community about the importance and availability of these three services. The specific directive given to the ASD was "fix these areas and fix them fast." In response, the ASD quickly hired additional staff for the emergency room services and to provide counseling and treatment to patients needing care for diabetes or obesity. In the rush to hire additional staff, little effort was made to inform the public of these services, so the result was that very talented new staff found themselves coming to work every day with not much to do. Once these new employees were hired, the ASD and executive team quickly switched their focus to other operational issues. As a result, over the next eighteen months the three areas did not see the increase in business to justify the additional headcount.

The fact that not much was happening in these three areas was certainly on the minds of some members of the executive team, but a climate of avoiding raising tough issues with the CEO fostered a reluctance in other executive staff to point out inconsistencies and challenge the manner in which business was being conducted, or the results being obtained. However, after a year and a half with no progress made in these three areas, the staff that had been hired became increasingly resentful and angry that their talents were being wasted. Several staff in both areas quit to take jobs in competing hospitals or organizations. Employees in other areas of the hospital began to voice their displeasure that they felt overloaded with work responsibilities while there were staff in the other areas "sitting around doing nothing." This led to some heated exchanges and the development of silos of distrust and uncooperativeness. Eventually, the lack of progress and increase in complaints and staff turnover brought the situation to a head, and the ASD was directed to act quickly to turn the situation around.

Thankfully, during the preceding six months, the human resources department at Angels of Mercy had introduced the conflict-to-cooperation training program to help address some ongoing issues with communication and to resolve other minor complaints. While the executive staff had not attended the training, the ASD and most other employees had. To her credit, the ASD reviewed the situation and discovered the oversight of having left out a strong community-outreach campaign. Rather than rush to "solving the problem" again, she decided to pull together a team of the key stakeholders and approach the opportunity from a positive perspective. This team consisted of the ASD, CEO, nursing director, marketing director, and a representative from emergency services, diabetes treatment, and obesity treatment. In addition, the ASD asked for two representatives from the community who served as directors of nonprofit healthcare services organizations to join the team.

The team met for a full-day planning session off-site to define the problem facing Angels of Mercy and the community, their respective concerns and goals, and to define a strategy or action plan for moving forward (see Figure 18). Those present at this planning session were impressed by the simplicity and effectiveness of the CCGA process, and it helped them see that unproductive conflict had been stifling growth, communication, and morale for the past year.

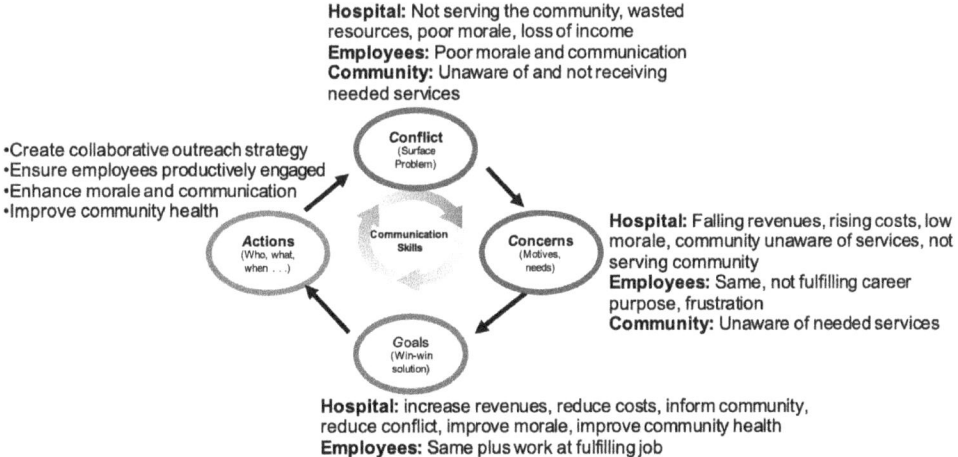

Figure 18: Angels of Mercy CCGA Diagram

As Figure 18 depicts, the team identified the problem from the various perspectives of the key stakeholders. At the planning session, the steering team began by revisiting the mission and values of Angels of Mercy, clarifying the type of working environment and relationships they would like to see enacted on a routine basis, and identifying the personal and business outcomes they would expect to see as a result of this effort. One of the outcomes of the planning session was for the CEO to recognize that he would need to learn to be less overbearing if he was to be trusted enough to get needed information quickly.

Following the planning session, this information was shared with all employees. Through emails and through periodic staff meetings, the CEO and ASD took time to meet with each department to explain the new strategy, standards for guiding behavior and conduct, desired outcomes, and benefits to all employees and clients. Time was also provided at these meetings to answer questions, take suggestions, and look for opportunities to improve the roll-out process.

The planning team also recognized that while most employees had attended the conflict-to-cooperation training, other staff, including the executive team, had not. To address this gap, they decided to conduct a series of workshops for all remaining employees and management. All employees, including management, attended the conflict-to-cooperation workshop held at their site. The content of the workshop was customized to include typical conflicts, problems, and issues which arose in the course of a normal work week. Participants actually diagnosed, mapped, and solved routine conflicts they experienced on the job during the course of the workshop. A second workshop for management and team leaders was held to teach more advanced coaching and facilitation skills. This workshop focused on improving the skills of these individuals to help run more effective meetings and resolve conflicts between management and employees, between peers, and with clients.

During the course of the workshops, the internal Angels of Mercy trainers and conflict-to-cooperation trainers sought additional opportunities to improve the quality of the case examples and interaction among participants. Within thirty days, all management and employees had completed the workshop, and managers and team leaders were utilizing the CCGA process in meetings. The steering team continued to meet twice a month to discuss progress and practice applying the CCGA process to upper-level conflicts, problems, and issues.

Over the next eighteen months, the hospital saw an increase in utilization of the services identified in the Community Health Assessment. As community information sessions and advertising were shared with the community, there was a slow but steady increase in the citizens coming to Angels of Mercy for additional care and treatment. As the success of these visits filtered back to the community, Angels of Mercy found that its reputation as the preferred local hospital to be admitted or treated dramatically improved.

This case illustrates the significant effects that a collaborative, cooperative work environment can have on business and personal productivity. As a result of implementing the conflict-mediation system, Angel of Mercy executive staff, management, and employees were able to look critically at their own behavior, business strategy, and opportunities to develop a new approach for turning the business around.

WHAT IF PEOPLE STILL CAN'T SOLVE CONFLICT THEMSELVES?

What happens when employees or managers have substantial disagreement on how to solve a conflict or respond to a potential opportunity? Or what should you do when two or more employees just can't seem to get along? In traditional work environments, employees tend to hope a manager or someone else will solve the problem. In this book, the authors recommend that you create a culture in which all employees have the skills to solve conflicts on their own whenever possible, and to seek assistance when needed.

There are a number of organizations that have developed very effective conflict-resolution processes. These include Morning Star (food processing), Buurtzorg (home healthcare), AES (energy), Whole Foods (supermarket), Patagonia (outdoor products), and others. Let's take a look at one of these organizations as most of these utilize a very similar process for addressing conflict at the lowest possible level.

Morning Star is the world's largest tomato-processing company and is located on the West Coast of the United States. The company was formed in 1970 when Chris Rufer started a one-person truck-driving business hauling tomatoes. Today, the business has grown to include harvesting tomatoes, a 200-plus-truck hauling business, and three high-technology food-processing plants, which produce over 40 percent of the tomato paste and diced tomato food products consumed in the United States. If you have eaten spaghetti or pizza sauce, ketchup, tomato paste, or diced tomatoes, then you have almost certainly enjoyed Morning Star's products on many occasions.

As described in Frederick Laloux's groundbreaking book, *Reinventing Organizations*, the values and standards of behavior and interaction for Morning Star's operations were put in place early in its history. When the first tomato-processing plant was built, Chris and the company's first employees met to define how they wanted to work together. They decided that two principles should inspire every management and interactive practice at the company. First, no one should ever use force against other people, and second, all employees should honor their commitments. These principles form the heart of Morning Star's conflict-resolution process.

The conflict-resolution process at Morning Star is called "Direct Communication and Gaining Agreement," and applies to any disagreement. The disagreement can vary from a simple difference of opinion about work tasks or responsibilities, to a breach of values or standards of behavior, performance issues, or even whether one employee feels another employee or manager is not doing their job or is doing it in an unfair manner. Whatever the topic, the individuals involved use the following process:

- The first step is for the two individuals to meet together to try and resolve the conflict or address the opportunity together. This can be accomplished following the CCGA process.
- If they can't reach a solution agreeable to both of them, they then agree on a colleague whom they both trust to act as a mediator or conflict coach. The colleague supports the parties in finding agreement but can't impose a solution.
- If this step does not succeed, a panel of topic-relevant colleagues is convened. This panel's role is to listen to and help shape an agreement with the two individuals. Like the colleague, the panel can't impose a decision or resolution, but generally those involved find that the moral weight of the panel is enough to help the two individuals come to a conclusion.

It is important to note that since the conflict or disagreement is private, all people involved are expected to respect confidentiality before, during, and after the process. This confidentiality applies to everyone. Thus, the intent of the process described above is for those involved to resolve the disagreement themselves, and everyone is discouraged from spreading the conflict by rumor-mongering, enlisting support from others, or building rival factions.

By examining this process above, the impact of a strong, respectful, skilled culture is evident. In traditional companies, when one person has a conflict with another, or one department has a problem with another department, they often complain but then leave it to someone "higher up" the hierarchy to do something about it. In organizations that have established engaging, respectful cultures in which employees are encouraged and supported to solve problems at the lowest possible level, people learn to step up and confront colleagues who harass, bully, belittle, or fail in their commitments.

CONCLUDING THOUGHTS

A group of children playing a game of basketball understands the value of defining the area of play, the rules of the game, roles and responsibilities as players, and what it means to "win." If children can learn and implement these concepts effectively, isn't it reasonable to expect those of us in formal organizations or associations to apply effective conflict skills as well? The conflict-mediation process provides an organization with the framework and skill sets for defining the playing field, roles, responsibilities, and outcomes expected in order to achieve individual and group success.

Does this mean that everyone always plays by the rules? Not at all; that is why the operating framework needs to be clearly articulated to everyone. We are all occasional transgressors. When we step "off the path," the principles and skills previously identified provide others with the ability to gently call it to our attention. As in sports, there are also those who are continual and intentional transgressors. When that happens, there are penalties, the option of retraining, and/or the alternative of leaving voluntarily or being asked formally to leave the game entirely.

We have suggested that healthcare organizations and their employees be thought of as sharing many characteristics with professional athletes. Athletes bring well-honed skills and knowledge, coupled with an understanding of the game process, and a commitment to engage productively with the team in order to perform well and win. As a result, they are handsomely paid and held up as public icons to be emulated. Executives, managers, employees, and volunteers in nonprofit organizations also bring their unique and very valuable knowledge and skills to their workplace. When this knowledge and skill is supported and encouraged through the application of standards for guiding conduct and behavior, a process for mediating their own conflicts, and the skills to communicate effectively, personal, group, and organizational success is enhanced, contributing to each individual's own personal and job satisfaction.

Conflict is an inevitable part of our lives, but conflict does not have to mean an all-out war, long-term discord, or diminished relationships. In *Mediation: Empowerment in Conflict Management*, Kathy Domenici (1996) observes that in mediating conflict the

> parties are not in a contest. The goal is not to find out who is right, who is to blame, or to whom to give credit. The goal is to find the appropriate resolution to the conflict, one that satisfies both parties.

When provided the right skills, a shared process for resolving conflicts, and the appropriate level of commitment, the level of unproductive conflict in your life, your team, and your organization can be diminished. By understanding and applying the conflict-mediation system, you can consistently turn conflict into an opportunity for cooperation.

The Least You Need to Remember

- Organizations can customize the conflict-mediation system to reflect their culture, values, and specific conflicts.
- The conflict-mediation system can be implemented in a work unit, department, division, or company-wide.
- When implementing on a broad scale, form a design team to provide guidance.
- Ensure that organizational standards for conduct and behavior are clear.
- Training can be provided to all employees and management.
- A roll-out plan will help ensure that the effort is implemented in a thoughtful manner.
- Any change or training effort will require some improvement.
- It is important to monitor and communicate the success of the effort. This will encourage the application and use of the conflict-mediation system.
- The conflict-mediation system is an effective means for turning conflict into opportunities for cooperation.

CHAPTER 6 TOOLS and ACTIVITIES

Implementation Process
- Which key stakeholders should be included on your steering team?
- Do you need sub-teams? If so, how many, and for what functions/sites?
- Does your organization have a set of standards or values for guiding conduct and behavior? If so, are they appropriate? If not, how can you develop these critical guidelines?
- Who will be trained and in what order?
- How will you introduce this process to management and employees?
- With what group will you pilot or test the conflict-mediation system? How will you incorporate needed changes to improve the training program?
- What is your plan for implementing the conflict-mediation system and training program throughout your organization?
- How do you plan on monitoring the impact of this effort and communicating the results to key stakeholders?

Chapter 7

MANAGING EVERYDAY CONFLICT

> *You are all busy. It's important to be busy, but*
> *if you don't find time to change the world,*
> *then you are busy keeping it the way it is.*
> —Robert Coles

In This Chapter

Although a great deal of conflict occurs at work between management and coworkers, we also experience conflict in other areas of our lives. In this chapter, we will explore how you may apply the conflict-mediation system to your personal, social, and community life. You will have the opportunity to examine a number of case examples that depict people resolving routine conflicts that occur in everyday interactions. As you read and study each example, we encourage you to consider the interaction from two perspectives. First, what would you do if you were one of the individuals involved? Second, consider each case from a coaching perspective. How would you coach these individuals through each conflict if asked?

Much of our waking time is spent at work, but conflict occurs in all lifestyles. In this chapter, we will describe how to apply this system with family, friends, and communities. You will also learn how the system can be useful even with those who are not familiar with the framework or skills.

FAMILY and CONFLICT MEDIATION

Family conflict has been present ever since Adam and Eve argued over who was to blame for eating the apple in the Garden of Eden. The ability of families to resolve conflict did not improve very much when you consider the story of their children, Cain and Abel. As discussed previously, conflict is a natural and inevitable condition that occurs when two or more individuals perceive that their goals, needs, or wants are in jeopardy of being frustrated by another. Conflicts within families can occur due to a wide range of conditions.

Life changes often cause stress that contributes to conflict within families, according to Thomas Holmes and Richard Rahe. These two psychologists studied 5,000 individuals to determine if there is a correlation between stress and illness. Their research showed a clear correlation between changes in health and significant change or stress in personal, family, or work situation. The table in Figure 19 summarizes the top twenty items they identified as major life-change events. According to Holmes and Rahe, each event's value reflects the event's life impact on the individual. The death of a spouse is assumed to be the most traumatic event with a point value of 100. Having a mortgage payment carries a lower point value of 31.

It is interesting to observe the list contains both negative events, such as death of a spouse or being fired at work, and positive events, such as marriage and addition of a new family member. It is also interesting to note that several of these life events may occur at the same time. For example, in the same year someone might have a parent pass away, lose their job, become ill, and then get into a new relationship and find a new place of employment. Collectively, these can cause great stress on the individual.

Rank	Life Event	Value
1	Death of spouse	100
2	Divorce	73
3	Marital separation	65
4	Jail term	63
5	Death of close family member	63
6	Personal injury or illness	53
7	Marriage	50
8	Fired at work	47
9	Marital reconciliation	45
10	Retirement	45
11	Change in health of a family member	44
12	Pregnancy	40
13	Sex difficulties	39
14	Addition of a new family member	39
15	Business readjustment	39
16	Change in financial state	38
17	Death of a close friend	37
18	Change in different line of work	36
19	Change in number of arguments with spouse	35
20	Mortgage	31

Figure 19: Life-Change Events

Conflicts in families do not have to be very traumatic to cause discord and unhappiness. In fact, many, if not most, conflicts occur over what we might consider to be relatively minor issues. Spouses and children often develop conflicts due to misunderstandings, unvoiced assumptions, or disagreements over roles or responsibilities. Conflicts may also occur when one individual means well, but is perceived by another as being inconsiderate. Consider the following case.

Steven is in the living room watching the television and ironing one of his wife's dresses as she returns from a trip to the supermarket.

"Hi, Lisa," he says. "Were you able to find everything okay?"

"Yeah, just about," she replies as she goes through the living room. "I couldn't find that pasta sauce we really like and . . ." She pauses as she sees the dress he is ironing.

"You didn't wash that dress, did you?" she asks as she puts down a bag of groceries.

Her husband beams. "I sure did. I washed the whole load of laundry, and I thought I'd iron a few of your items because I know how much you hate ironing."

Lisa explodes, "I can't believe you were so stupid as to wash and iron a silk dress! Didn't you read the label?"

"But it was in the laundry basket and—" Steven begins.

"You just ruined my favorite dress. I can't believe you did something so brainless. Why don't you stick to what you do best and just watch TV!" she says as she drops the other bag of groceries on the kitchen table, storms off to their bedroom, and slams the door.

Steven wads the dress up and throws it in the corner. "You're welcome!" he yells. "See if I ever help out around the house again!"

Some of you can probably identify with this scenario. Others may be thinking, "Are you kidding? I'd be glad if my spouse just washed a load of laundry or ironed their clothes once in a while." Poor laundering skills did not show up on the major life-event scale that Holmes and Rahe developed, but it is often the "little" life events that cause discord among family members. Family members have disagreements about home chores, allowances, who gets to use the car, what is for dinner, whose turn it is to clean the litter box, how long one person has been on the phone, when homework should be done, and what time the kids need to be home from a date.

Regardless of the source, the conflict-mediation system can be used to help defuse and resolve these frequent points of contention. For example, in the scenario above, Steve meant well, but ruined one of Lisa's favorite dresses. Lisa responded very negatively by attacking Steven personally. Suppose we revisit this scenario and observe how this situation might be handled between someone who understands the process and someone who does not. This time, assume Lisa has been through the conflict-mediation process training at her job and sees an opportunity to apply those skills with Steven.

Steven is in the living room watching a movie and ironing one of his wife's dresses as she returns from a trip to the supermarket.

"Hi, Lisa," he says. "Were you able to find everything okay?"

"Yeah, just about," she replies as she goes through the living room. "I couldn't find that pasta sauce we really like and . . ." She pauses as she sees the dress he is ironing.

"You didn't wash that dress, did you?" she asks as she puts down a bag of groceries.

Her husband beams. "I sure did. I washed the whole load of laundry, and now I am ironing a few of your items because I know how much you hate ironing."

Lisa sighs, "Steven, I appreciate that you are trying to do something nice. Did you know that the dress you washed and are ironing is made from silk?"

"No, is that important?" Steven responds.

"Yes," she says. "Silk needs to be dry-cleaned. Washing it and running it through the dryer has probably caused it to shrink and lose its shape. I doubt I can wear it again, and that was one of my favorite dresses. This is the second time you've ruined one of my outfits, and I think we need to talk so it does not happen again."

"Well, I was just trying to be nice. You're the one who put the dress in the laundry basket, so how was I to know it couldn't be washed?" Steven replies defensively.

"Look, Steven, I am disappointed, but I am not angry with you," she says. "I appreciate what you tried to do, and I want to figure out how to keep this from happening again. When you ruin something of mine, it makes me angry, and I hate wasting money."

"Okay," Steven says. "So what do you suggest? Do you want me to just never wash or iron again?"

Lisa replies, smiling, "Nice try, but you don't get out of housework forever."

Lisa thinks for a moment and then says, "I think it's safe to say we both want our clothes cleaned correctly. Is that right?"

"Sure," Steven says.

"So, if you do the laundry, can't you read the labels and see which ones are not machine-washable?" Lisa offers.

"Look, these all look the same to me. After all, I do sort them by whites and solids already," he counters. "Why not put them in different piles—those that need to be washed and those that need to be dry-cleaned?"

"Yeah, I could get another clothes basket and we put the regular laundry in one and the clothes to be dry-cleaned in the other," she suggests.

"I think that will work," Steven replies sheepishly. "I suppose I can tell the difference between a basket full of regular laundry and dry-cleaning."

"That's fine," Lisa says. "But if you are not sure, either read the label or don't wash the item at all, okay?"

"Yes," he says. "If in doubt, I won't wash any of your stuff."

"Well, you finish ironing and put up the groceries while I go back to the store and get a second clothes basket right now!" Lisa laughs.

If Lisa and Steven had visually diagrammed the conflict using the CCGA process, it would probably look like the information in Figure 20 below:

Figure 20: Household Chores CCGA Diagram

In this scenario, Lisa and Steven are able to mediate the conflict to an agreeable solution. Lisa took the lead in identifying the problem and expressing her concerns and desired outcomes. Note that Lisa relied on her communication skills in following the CCGA mediation process. She let Steven know that she did not want any more clothes ruined, explored alternatives, and agreed on some actions they both can take.

The ability to communicate effectively and mediate conflicts within a family is very important. Recall the first scenario in which both Lisa and Steven become angry and the result is unproductive conflict. Consider how much more unproductive the conflict would have been had children been present. Children learn to model the behavior of their parents. If parents are able to model effective communication and problem-solving skills, children also learn and employ those skills.

CONFLICTS with FRIENDS

Conflicts don't just happen at work and within the family; they also happen between friends or neighbors. Relationships between friends and neighbors are very important. Friends are individuals with whom we can share our thoughts, concerns, and desires. They are often people we can count on to provide advice and support. Similarly, neighbors are the people who live nearby. As with our friends, we socialize with them, let our children play with their children, visit each other's homes, and depend on each other for occasional supplies or tools. It is sad and unpleasant when two friends or neighbors have petty conflicts that escalate unnecessarily. Consider the following scenario.

Bob and Carol have lived across the street from Jim and Mary since they moved to the neighborhood three years ago. Bob and Carol have one child, a girl who is six. Jim and Mary have two children, ages seven and nine. The neighbors get along very well, although Bob has noticed that Jim seems much more interested in work and golf than in his children. One morning, Carol and Mary have gone shopping, and Bob is getting ready to go jogging with his daughter. Bob and his daughter like these times because he can push her in a baby jogger through the park and they often stop to feed the ducks. As he is lacing up his shoes, there is a knock on the door. When Bob goes to the door, his neighbor's two children are standing there.

"Good morning," Bob says. "What are you two doing today?"

The oldest says, "Dad is going golfing and he asked us to come over here until Mom gets back."

Bob looks up at the sound of a car engine and sees Jim beginning to back out of his driveway. "Hey, Jim," Bob yells as he walks over to the car. "What's going on?"

"Well, I saw you were home and figured you could watch the kids while I go golfing," says Jim.

"I really can't right now, Jim," explains Bob. "I'm going jogging with my daughter and can't watch your kids."

"Come on, you can wait until the girls get back from shopping," snorts Jim. "Besides, the kids love playing over at your house."

Bob is beginning to get a bit angry. "Jim, I'm sorry, but I can't watch your kids now. When I get back from jogging, I'll be glad to watch them, but not now."

Jim glares at Bob and says, "Okay, fine! You go jogging and I'll just wait here. But hurry because I don't want to wait too long to get out on the course!"

Your initial reaction is probably that Jim is behaving rather thoughtlessly. Unfortunately, that is often how conflicts begin. Like many minor events, this one could become a seed of discontent and mistrust that serves to poison a positive relationship between neighbors. Care should be taken because the relationship is more than that between Bob and Jim. The relationships also include their wives and children.

Below in Figure 21 is a CCGA worksheet that illustrates how this situation could be visually diagramed for both Jim and Bob.

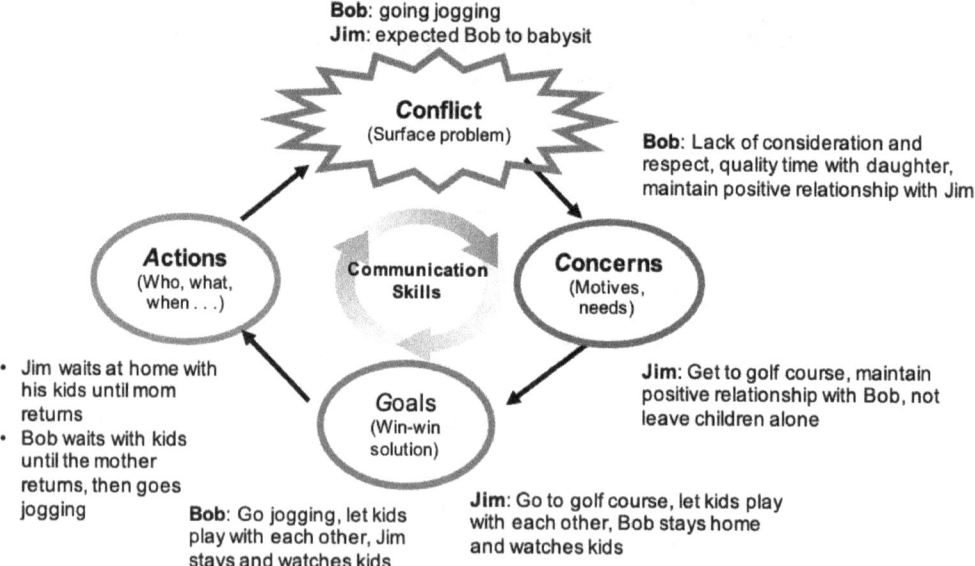

Figure 21: Friends CCGA Diagram

Compare what you identified with the following. Jim's position is that he wants Bob to watch his children while he goes golfing. Bob's position is that he wants to go jogging with his daughter.

What might be their concerns? Jim is concerned with getting to the golf course, and Bob is concerned with spending some quality time with his daughter and avoiding being imposed upon.

What might be their respective goals for a positive outcome? For Jim, it might be that Bob stay home and watch the children while he goes golfing, maintaining a good relationship with Bob and giving his children some time to play with Bob's daughter. Bob would also like to maintain a good relationship with Jim, but go jogging with his daughter.

What actions might be considered? Jim could put off golfing until later in the day, some other day, or take his children with him to the golf course (they might really enjoy riding around on the golf cart). Bob could put off running until Jim or the wives return, not go jogging at all, or just go jogging with his daughter. Can you think of any other options?

The desired outcome of this episode is to avoid having a little thoughtlessness blow up into a major event and destroy a friendship. At different times in our lives we are all a bit thoughtless.

By focusing on the facts, at least Jim and Bob can reach some resolution to the conflict. If Bob is able to communicate his position and concerns effectively, he may help Jim see that his assumption that Bob would just watch the children is thoughtless.

CONFLICT MEDIATION and COMMUNITY GROUPS

We are all members of various groups such as synagogues, churches, PTAs, booster clubs, sports, and scouting associations, just to name a few. Others among us serve as board members or volunteers for nonprofit and other community-based organizations. Occasionally, differences in opinions, strategies, and priorities lead to conflict, which can cause one of these organizations to self-destruct, despite the fact that these organizations have beneficial missions.

In chapter five, you saw a case example in which two board members of a nonprofit organization were in disagreement over which goals should take precedence during the coming year. In this example, Linda, the executive director, was able to work with these two individuals to begin a process of dialogue. This example is not uncommon. Nonprofits and community-based groups experience as much conflict as any organization. Whether you are planning a car wash, bake sale, overnight band trip, or major funding event, there is bound to be conflict throughout the process. Let's look at an example of a conflict that occurs between a group of parent volunteers assisting with their children's pending band trip.

Background

Amy is chair of the parent committee that is assisting the band teacher to plan for an upcoming competition which will take place in a city several hundred miles away. One of the tasks to be accomplished is arranging for a bus to take the children and their equipment to the competition. Rose, one of the other mothers, has volunteered to arrange for the transportation. Over the past few months, the parent committee has met several times. Each time, Rose reports that she is "looking into the transportation," but with a week to go, she still has not obtained a contract. Amy has decided to call Rose and see if she can get to the bottom of this issue.

"Hello, Rose? This is Amy with the parent committee," Amy says when Rose answers the phone.

"Hi, Amy! What can I do for you?" Rose replies.

"Amy, I am calling about the bus contract for the upcoming band trip," Amy begins. "Listen, I know we have been around this already, but I really need to get closure on this topic. I am feeling very uneasy because we only have one week before the band trip, and a contract with the bus has not been obtained. We should have had the contract approved two weeks ago. I'd like to know what you think."

Rose replies, "Well, I have already told you I am working on it."

"Rose," Amy says, "I think we have a problem. We should already have a bus contract and we don't. Do you agree?"

"Yes," Rose answers. "But I am talking with a bus company this week. Besides, I have been busy traveling for my company."

"Rose, I can appreciate how difficult it is to work on this project when you are traveling," Amy notes. "I am also aware that if we do not have a bus contract approved within the next three days, the kids will not be able to go on the trip. I am concerned that they will be very disappointed because they have been practicing for months. Further, the band director has put his faith in us to get the trip set up. Do you feel this way too?"

"Sure, but I think we will get the bus," Rose offers. "I kind of do everything at the last minute, but it all gets done. That's just my style."

"I can see how that style works very well for many people," Amy observes. "And we have a project plan that you helped develop. According to the plan, we should have the contract already. My goal is to come to an agreement with you now that will ensure that we have a clear understanding on who will do what to make sure that the bus contract is obtained in the next two days. This way we will have the last major task completed and can formally announce to the kids and band director that the trip is ready to go. Would you agree with this goal, or do you have any others?"

"No, that sounds fine to me," Rose agrees. "But what do you propose?"

Amy says, "First, can you tell me which bus company has the best rate, meets the school criteria for safety, and has a bus available?"

"Actually, both ABC Bus Enterprises and Nationwide Bus Service have comparable rates and have been used by the school district for band and sports events," Rose replies.

"Do they both have buses available on the day we need them?" Amy persists.

Rose pauses. "I am not sure, but I can call and find out."

"Okay," Amy says. "Can I ask that you call right now and see which company has a bus available? Also, will you ask that they scan and email a contract to you and me immediately?"

"Sure," says Rose. "I'll call right now and call you back as soon as I have talked with them."

"That would be great," Amy replies. "And I want to reiterate how important it is that we complete this task since everything else really depends on getting the bus. If you find you don't have time to call today and get back with me, I would like to take responsibility for getting this done myself. Would that be okay?"

"Yes, but I promise I will get this done today," Rose responds. "It should have been done earlier and I just let it go too long."

"Great," says Amy. "I appreciate your willingness to help get this task completed. I also know the kids will be very grateful. I will look forward to your call in the next hour or so."

If you have ever been in Amy's position, you know that this is not a very comfortable conversation. Dealing with other volunteers is very different from dealing with coworkers or subordinates who are being paid to get a job done. Let's look at Figure 22, which displays how this case might be mapped.

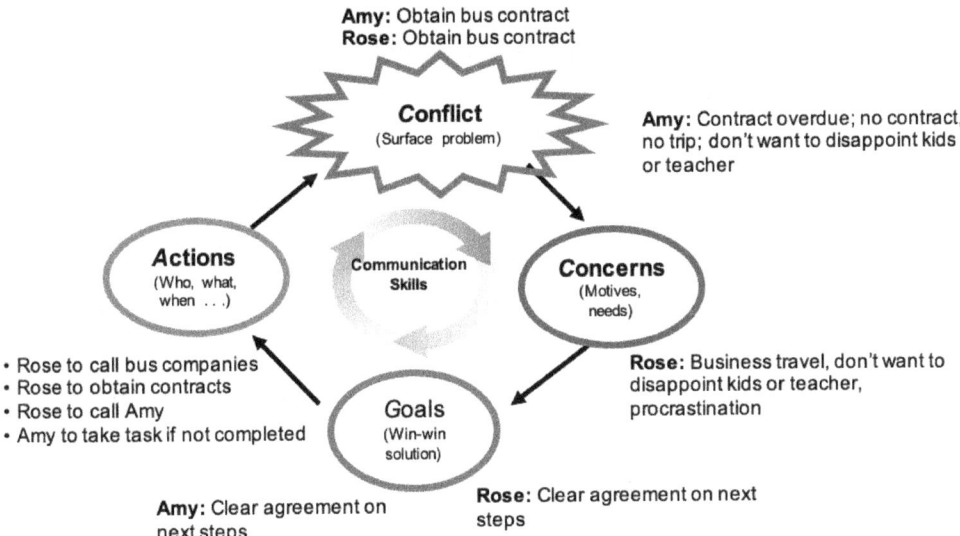

Figure 22: Volunteers CCGA Diagram

What was the conflict? The conflict in this case was that a bus contract had not been obtained with only a few days to go before the band trip. Both Amy and Rose came to an agreement on this point fairly quickly.

What were their concerns? Amy's concerns were that the contract was well overdue, and if a bus is not obtained, the band trip will not happen. This would result in disappointing the children who have been practicing for this event as well as disappointing the band director who needs the support of the parent volunteers. Rose observed that she had not completed the task due to business travel, but like Amy, she did not want to disappoint the children or band director.

What were their goals? Both Amy and Rose agreed that the goal to be agreed upon was developing a clear understanding of who was going to do what next in order to confirm the bus contract.

What was the action plan? The action plan which Amy and Rose agreed to was that Rose would call the two bus companies, find out if a bus was available on the correct date, and then ask that a copy of the contract be faxed or emailed to either Rose or Amy. Further, Rose will be calling Amy within the next hour to give her an update. Note that given the short time frame, and importance of this task, Amy has added another action—if Rose can't get the job done today, Amy will take over the task.

It is unfortunate when political agendas, false impressions, micromanagement, or misunderstandings cause these groups to become dysfunctional. When members within these groups become dysfunctional, the damage, stress, and unpleasantness erode the effective use of resources, funds, time, and energy. When a group lacks the ability to consistently mediate its own conflict, morale suffers, turnover and absenteeism soar, customer service is eroded, and productivity nosedives. But the impact goes well beyond the group to the surrounding community. Children, families, funding sources, and supporters all suffer as well. As you have just seen, the conflict-mediation system provides an effective framework for assisting organizations, work teams, and volunteers to focus on providing important services to the community—not spending its valuable time and resources bickering with each other.

The Least You Need to Remember

- Life changes cause stress that contributes to conflict.
- The conflict-mediation system is an effective tool for addressing conflicts in families, friends, social groups, and community settings.
- As in a work setting, it is helpful to visually map or diagram the conflict using the CCGA process. This helps everyone understand the nature of the conflict and enhances the opportunities for success.

CHAPTER 7 TOOLS and ACTIVITIES

I. Life-Events Worksheet

At the beginning of this chapter you learned about the "major life events" table developed by Thomas Holmes and Richard Rahe. As you will recall, this table depicts a number of major life events that can influence the level of stress occurring in one's life. Review the worksheet below and place an *X* opposite those situations that currently impact your life. This list is by no means complete. Space is provided at the end of the list for you to add other significant life events that you may encounter.

Life-Change Events

Event	Value	Present in my life
Death of spouse	100	_____
Divorce	75	_____
Marital separation	65	_____
Jail term	63	_____
Death of a close family member	63	_____
Personal injury or illness	53	_____
Marriage	50	_____
Dismissal from work	47	_____
Marital reconciliation	45	_____
Retirement	45	_____
Change in health of family member	44	_____
Pregnancy	40	_____
Sexual dysfunction	39	_____
Addition of a new family member	39	_____
Business readjustment	39	_____
Change in financial status	38	_____
Death of close friend	37	_____
Change to different profession	36	_____
Change in # of arguments with spouse	36	_____
Major mortgage payments	31	_____
Foreclosure of mortgage or loan	30	_____
Change in responsibilities at work	29	_____
Son or daughter leaving home	29	_____
Trouble with in-laws	29	_____
Outstanding personal achievement	28	_____
Partner begins or stops work	26	_____
Begin or end school	26	_____
Change in living conditions	25	_____
Major change in personal habits	24	_____
Trouble with supervisor	23	_____
Change in work hours or conditions	20	_____
Change residence/schools/recreation	19	_____
Change in social activities	18	_____
Small mortgage or loan	17	_____
Change in sleeping/eating habits	16	_____
Change in # of family get-togethers	15	_____
Vacation	13	_____
Major holiday	12	_____
Minor violations of the law	11	_____
Other event		_____
Other event		_____

Interpretation

Don't attempt to add up a "score" on this scale. The values are there simply to show the *relative* impact of stressful events and to give some indication of the wide range of stressors in our lives. The greater the amount of change and stress in your life, the more likely one will also experience increased levels of conflict. By being aware of the stressors in your life, you can monitor your behavior and reactions to these events. You may want to focus on reducing stress in one or more areas in order to achieve greater balance in your life.

1. What were the top three stressors in your life?
2. What impact are they having on your well-being? Is the impact positive, negative, or both?
3. Are these stressors causing more or less conflict in your life? Why?
4. What can you do to achieve greater balance and reduce stress in your life?

II. Personal-Conflict Diagram

Take a few minutes to think about some of the relationships you have with friends, family, or community associates. Identify a conflict, problem, or misunderstanding that is occurring. Take a few minutes to diagram how you might approach this conflict in order to achieve an effective resolution.

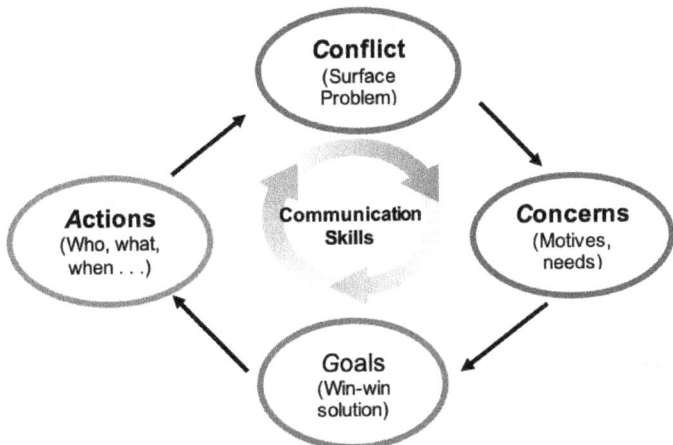

Chapter 8
TAKING THE NEXT STEP

Organizations could accomplish so much more if they relied on the passion evoked when we connect to others, purpose to purpose. So many of us want to be more. So many of us hunger to discover what we might become together.
—M. Wheatley and M. Kellner-Rogers

The general rule seems to be that the level of consciousness of an organization cannot exceed the level of consciousness of its leader.
—Frederic LaLoux

In This Chapter

In this final chapter, you will learn that the ability to communicate and address conflict effectively is a key skill that leaders need to develop if they are to progress in today's demanding healthcare work environment. When managers and employees are supported and encouraged through the application of standards for guiding conduct and behavior, a process for mediating their own conflicts, and the skills to communicate effectively, personal, group, and organizational success is significantly enhanced.

There is a great quote by Simon Sinek in his Ted Talk in which he states, "People don't buy *what* you do—they buy *why* you do it." This Ted Talk centers around the idea of culture, why it is important, and how to build an effective organizational culture by focusing on answering your company's *"why."* Sinek stresses that answering this question first leads to other questions:

- What do you stand for?
- What are your core values?
- What's your team like?
- How do you interact together?
- How do you attract and keep great people?
- How do you provide the very best service or develop the best products over the long term?

Today, more than ever, healthcare organizations are striving to answer those questions and build a culture that brings and retains top-level talent to provide the best patient care or develop the best healthcare products or services possible. So, as more and more companies focus on this, what will be the impact? How will this change business as we know it? To build on what Sinek said above, we believe employees want to have more than just a job or a place to come to work. They want to be engaged and to bring their full self to the workplace every day! We believe that we have identified four trends that will continue to drive the need for flexible, respectful cultures that go beyond rhetoric and truly "walk the walk." The bottom line is that the very best organizations rely on great leaders and employees at *all levels* to get work done effectively. To sum up what we have been trying to convey in this book, we believe that your success as a healthcare organization is strongly influenced by your ability to ensure a culture of effective communication, collaboration, flexibility, and an engaging employee experience.

EFFECTIVE COMMUNICATION

In *Reinventing Organizations,* Frederic Laloux observes that almost everyone recognizes that the way we run organizations today no longer works. Survey after survey clearly illustrates that despite the superficial efforts to appeal to the workforce in organizations, most employees are not engaged at work. To reiterate, the most recent worldwide Gallup poll on engagement indicates that over 87 percent of employees are not engaged when they come to work.

Think of how this statistic translates to your organization. What does it mean if over 80 percent of your employees are just coming to work, doing their job, and leaving their passion and enthusiasm at home? It should be very clear that employees view their work today not just as a "job," but rather as a place to find meaning and achieve their life purpose. For most employees, work is no longer constrained to a cubicle or a desk; it is an opportunity to learn, to share ideas, work in teams, and serve patients or develop the best services and products possible. They want to contribute to something bigger than themselves with others. What a wonderful shared purpose!

Communication is a very powerful tool that can have a massive impact on the success of any healthcare organization. Effective communication can increase employee engagement, boost workplace productivity, and drive business growth. Communication is the cornerstone of an engaged workforce. A healthcare organization's workforce represents its most significant investment and ultimately determines its success or failure. Engaged employees are far more likely to demonstrate the dedication and commitment that are essential to the long-term growth of any company, large or small. One of the most difficult challenges for any organization today is to find ways to effectively speak to its employees and enable them to interact effectively with each other.

COOPERATION

Healthcare organizations must also learn to honestly evaluate how their organization interacts with potential talent, current employees, and the work itself to create an environment of cooperation. Cooperation is key to aligning how work gets done across your institution, how care is provided to patients, how effectively technology is utilized, and the quality of your products and services. How well your organization cooperates should not be left to chance.

To tackle this, healthcare organizations must clearly define what cooperation means for their employees, the right tools to use, what skills are needed, and how to deploy them in the most effective manner. Cooperative workplaces also need to move beyond proximity-based parameters (common areas) in order to encourage communication across departments, professional specialties, and perhaps even across geographical, cultural, and hierarchical realities.

FLEXIBILITY

A study conducted by Ernst and Young found that 76 percent of employees find it difficult to manage personal, family, and work commitments. This is a primary reason why workplace flexibility along with compensation and benefits are the top considerations for most people considering a job or staying with an employer. With over 78 percent of millennials being part of dual-career couples, a parent is more likely to take time off to care for their children. However, maternity/paternity leaves are limited in most organizations, and parents cannot forego the care of their child once they exhaust their time off. This is why flextime and telecommuting are becoming almost a precondition for employees.

Workplace flexibility today isn't just a "good-to-have perk" anymore; it's good business sense. Organizational culture experts have long maintained that employees given flexibility and freedom not only tend to outperform their clock-punching counterparts but are also happier and healthier both in their professional and personal lives. By embracing flexibility, organizations can drive productivity and also manage to get a handle on the skyrocketing cost of healthcare.

EMPLOYEE EXPERIENCE

Each year, millions of people across the globe go to Disney theme parks. The reason is simple—visitors consistently rate the trip as one of the best customer experiences they have had in their lives. And you can bet this is not an accident. Disney works hard and continually to ensure that the customer experience is nothing short of superb.

With the consumerization of the workplace, the measure of the "best" organizations is now the total experience of the *employee*. Company-review sites like Glassdoor, where employees can rate and review their employers based on compensation, benefits, management, or organizational culture, have made it critical for organizations to consider employee experience seriously. What this means is that your healthcare organization needs to be very proactive in providing the best experience to your employees.

Moreover, healthcare organizations must ensure that their culture is conducive to creating a desirable identity for themselves. With analytics enabling healthcare organizations to map various touchpoints within employee experience, employers are better equipped to predict, manage, and measure the impact of their employee-experience initiatives.

The future of work has arrived, and companies can't afford to ignore it. Substantial changes in workplace technology, workforce demographics, and employee preference are transforming the workplace. By cultivating a deeper relationship with employees through effective collaboration, communication, and providing flexibility and a great employee experience, healthcare organizations can fundamentally alter the way their employees view work and create a culture in which they are able to identify and address conflicts and opportunities quickly.

CONFLICT and GROWTH

As you have experienced firsthand, the prospect of engaging in conflict frequently scares and alarms people. In the classic four stages of team growth (forming, storming, norming, and performing), the second stage deals specifically with the group's ability to deal with and overcome conflict, and the third stage relates to how well the group can develop norms or standards of behavior that can lead to high performance. Many groups never become fully functioning teams, work units, or departments, and many organizations never break out of mediocrity because the members shy away from the "storming" stage. These teams and organizations fear and avoid conflict and consequently fail to develop the skills and create the processes, structures, and integrity needed to turn conflict into a positive opportunity for sharing new ideas, taking risks, and experimenting. As a result, these organizations and teams never attain the third stage of team growth—developing norms in which they work collaboratively to develop a culture that fosters deep trust, effective communication, accountability, critical introspection, and other elements that drive organizational success. Instead, these work units, teams, departments, and organizations settle for sub-optimal norms; they say publicly how they value transparency, respect, and open communication, but in practice they spread rumors, talk about colleagues behind their backs, and avoid conflict like a plague.

This is true of interpersonal relationships as well. We often limit the richness of our personal relationships with friends, neighbors, and family members by establishing boundaries to our interaction simply to avoid conflict. Admittedly, some conflict experiences are so negative that any indication that a new conflict might be headed our way leads us to try and sidestep or avoid the experience altogether. However, we also can all learn better ways, enhanced perspectives, skills, and tools to address conflict productively and respectfully. In this book, you have been provided with an abundance of information and resources, including new tools and insight to form a solid foundation for building your mastery of conflict management.

The only way teams, couples, and organizations can achieve truly high performance is when people are able to identify and address conflict professionally and respectfully. Diversity of perspective and expertise has to emerge for groups and organizations to achieve the highest levels of decision-making. That diverse sharing depends on members feeling safe enough to be open to other ideas and conflict. Team, family, or organizational members must believe it is okay for you see something one way, for someone else to see it another way, and that the best solution might be a combination of both. Keeping a focus on ideas instead of personalities can be a challenge. It takes awareness, commitment, and skill—all of which can be developed through the application of the principles presented in this book.

The Least You Need to Remember

> ➢ The ability to address conflicts in a constructive manner is a crucial skill for anyone in today's busy work world.
>
> ➢ The conflict-mediation system is an effective means for turning conflict into opportunities for cooperation.

CHAPTER 8 TOOLS and ACTIVITIES

Conversations about Culture

A proactive approach to conflict includes not just developing the personal skills to respond to conflict, but also recognizing opportunities to make improvements where needed. Executive teams and work teams can achieve this goal by periodically addressing questions:

- Do our institutional (or work team) vision/mission statements reflect a commitment to treating each other with respect, civility, and care?
- Do we have clear norms of acceptable behavior that outline how we expect to interact with each other, our customers, and the community?
- Have we developed safe and respectful processes for holding oneself and others accountable for these norms?
- Do we have clear, transparent processes for reporting harassment, discrimination, incivility, and disrespect?
- What evidence is there that clearly indicates that we are fully supporting these items above? What evidence is there that we are not supporting these desired outcomes?

Empathizing with Others

The ability to address conflict with another individual is influenced by how well you can empathize with that person. "Empathy" is the unique human ability to feel the emotions that another individual is feeling. For example, if someone accidentally hits their thumb with a hammer, we can empathize by saying, "Ouch! I've done that. It really hurts, doesn't it?"

It is often important to take time to empathize with another individual or group with whom you are in conflict. An effective exercise for helping understand and empathize with others is the "compassion exercise." To engage in this powerful activity, focus your attention on the other individual or group and say the following to yourself:

Just like me, he/she/they are seeking happiness in their life.

Just like me, he/she/they are seeking to avoid suffering in their life.

Just like me, he/she/they have known loneliness, sadness, lack of trust, and despair.

Just like me, he/she/they are seeking to meet their own needs.

Just like me, he/she/they are learning about life and trying to create connections.

Saying these simple words will help create a greater awareness of the connection between you and the other individual or group, and help establish a positive perspective for addressing any conflict.

Assess Your Willingness to Act

Take a few minutes to carefully consider the following questions:

Is unproductive conflict having a negative impact upon your personal, family, or work life? If so, what is the evidence?

Are you willing to use the knowledge and skill presented in this book to address this conflict productively?

Where will you start? Select one conflict that you feel can be addressed constructively and map out the conflict using the illustration below.

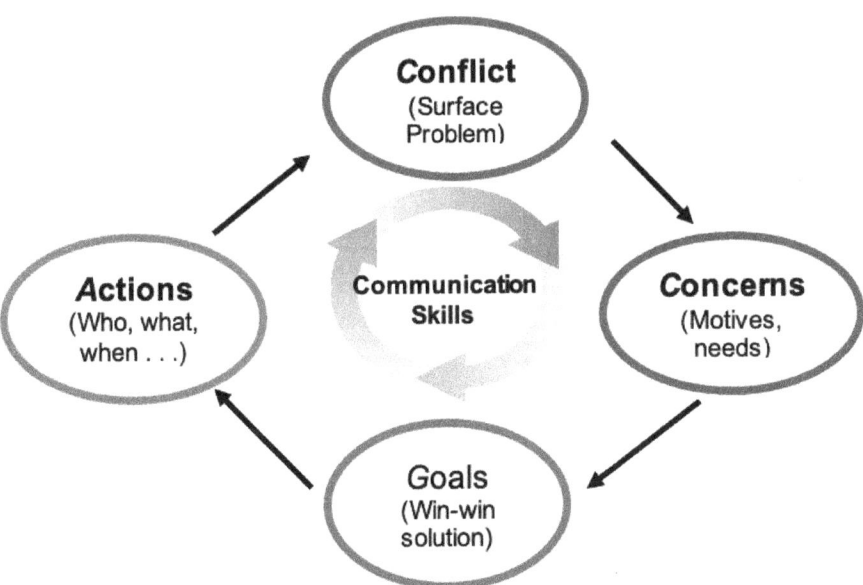

Reflect on What You Learned

Individually and/or as a group, review the quotes posted at the beginning of each chapter.

Based on what you have learned in this book and where you hope your healthcare organization goes in the future, what do these quotes tell you now?

Did certain quotes inspire or challenge you more than others? If so, why?

Do you have favorite quotes of your own that have great meaning to you? What are they, and why do you find them inspiring or insightful? How do these relate to your work in healthcare?

CONFLICT CASES

Case #1: Transitioning to a New Director

Tranquil Times Retirement Center (TTRC) is in the middle of a change. The past director, Brad Johnson, was a laid-back, relaxed administrator. He had been the director of TTRC for over twelve years and had become very comfortable not only in his position but with center staff as well. During this period, business had been great for TTRC with a solid base of residents and a steady stream of couples or individuals seeking a place to retire. Residents, nurses, doctors, and other employees admired Director Johnson for his willingness to empower them to "do the right thing" and maintain the high standards of quality that TTRC had come to know.

Unfortunately, the economy has begun a downward spiral, and this trend begins to affect TTRC. Even though the center has a great reputation, residency has declined somewhat as more and more potential new residents are choosing to stay in their homes or to live with relatives. The CEO of TTRC pressured Brad to decrease costs and institute a new campaign to attract more residents. Brad did not feel up to this challenge at this point in his career and opted to retire earlier than anyone expected.

The CEO instituted a search for a new center director and hired Amy Wilson. Amy has experience in the profession but is new to TTRC. She also wants to prove her abilities as the new director and make immediate changes that will impress the CEO. In her first week on the job, she begins reducing costs by not authorizing some supply purchases and cutting back on the number of hours employees can work. She also begins enforcing very strict rules for behavior and the dress code, sets new designated times for resident meals and other activities, and has written up a few employees for minor infractions. In addition, she has begun posting productivity results publicly, which has caused embarrassment for some areas of TTRC.

The employees are beginning to really tire of the constant

micromanaging and oversight that Amy is now bringing to TTRC. Several people have begun looking for work elsewhere, and it is not uncommon to hear someone stay, "This is just not a fun place to work at anymore!" Many residents are also beginning to comment on their lack of understanding for the changes being implemented.

Your Role: As the assistant director of TTRC, you understand the demands being placed on the center to reduce costs and are concerned about the methods Amy has instituted to try and turn things around. How can you use the CCGA model in a one-to-one meeting with Amy to help improve the situation?

Case #2: Call-Center Quandary

Mercy General Hospital is facing a very challenging problem with employee absenteeism among certified nurse assistants, patient-transport specialists, and other nursing support positions. The problem has become so bad that on some weekends and during holidays, 28 percent of the individuals in these positions call in sick. As the human resources administrator for Mercy General Hospital, you estimate that absenteeism is costing the facility over $12,500 per month. In addition, employees who are showing up for work are getting tired at having to cover not only their jobs but also the jobs of those employees who are absent. Many of these employees are beginning to voice their desire to begin looking for a job with a competitor.

You have conducted a little research on the internet to see what other hospitals have done to try to deal with this problem. One option really appeals to you, and you put it in place. This option is to give a bonus to employees who show up for work each week. To be fair, you have established a lottery where the names of these employees who were at work are put in a box, and once a week, you pick a name from the box, and that employee gets a prize of a $250 gift card.

Your plan has been in effect now for six months, and it has achieved amazing results. Absenteeism has dropped from 28 to 7 percent. Unfortunately, while this bonus plan has achieved the desired result of reduced absenteeism, it has created another problem: sick employees who are coming into work to add their name to the lottery. These individuals are spreading illness to other workers, and it is clearly unsafe for patients.

Your Role: How can you apply the CCGA model with this group of employees to revisit the problem of absenteeism and/or a method for rewarding attendance in a manner that is fair, healthy, and has the support of those involved?

Case #3: New Nurse Supervisor

Biltmore Hospital's nursing department is undergoing a major transition. The past nurse supervisor was a superb manager and leader. She did a great job and was admired by everyone. Her reputation as an outstanding administrator was well known in the healthcare community, and a rival hospital made her an offer she could not refuse. While everyone was glad to see her get this impressive pay raise and good job, they were very sorry to see her go.

The VP of operations selected her replacement without any input from the employees of this department. The new nursing supervisor comes in like a tidal wave. She immediately begins to change schedules, procedures, and demands staff take on new roles and responsibilities without any discussion at all and without trying to understand the work of the department. In addition, she is brash and rude in meetings, publicly embarrasses employees, is aggressive, and sets unrealistic deadlines. She also makes negative comments about the previous nursing supervisor and makes it clear that she thinks the department had been terribly mismanaged.

You have talked to several employees who all feel that the new nursing supervisor is very unprofessional, a micromanager, and have expressed their intention to leave as soon as they can find another job. Everyone feels bullied and demeaned by this new supervisor. You love your job, but you are also tired with this treatment.

Your Role: Use the CCGA model on your own to reflect upon how this challenge might be addressed if you approach the nursing supervisor with your concerns and observations. Whom else would you approach and discuss the situation with using the CCGA model?

Case #4: Falling Asleep on the Job

Linda is a nurse who has worked at St. Elmo's Children's Hospital for the past seven years in the physical rehabilitation department. Linda has a child who is autistic and occasionally acts in very inappropriate and violent ways when he is frustrated. While Linda has assistance to manage her son's needs during the workday, she has little to no assistance on the weekends or after work hours.

Linda's supervisor and colleagues have noticed that during the last year, Linda has been coming to work late and leaving thirty minutes early almost every day. In addition, while she is at work, she often snores in her cubicle. Her supervisor and colleagues have mentioned to her that she is falling asleep and have expressed concern for her health and well-being. When asked by her colleagues why she is late and having a hard time staying awake, Linda says she has sleep apnea and has a C-pap machine but does not want to use it as it is uncomfortable and the noise keeps her awake.

The nurses finally ask the supervisor to intervene. Their position is that they have to do their job, and now they are expected to cover for Linda too.

Your Role: Use the CCGA model to plan a meeting with Linda to address this problem. Are there others who should be present at this meeting? If so, who and why?

Case #5: Unprofessional Behavior

Stacy Boyle is a phlebotomist at Hilltop Medical Center. On this particular day, she is asked to draw blood on a comatose patient for routine tests. As she enters the patient's room, she knocks, announces herself, informs the patient why she is there, and then verifies that this is the right patient. She then puts a tourniquet on his arm, swabs the area with alcohol, and prepares to insert the needle. Just as she says, "I am going to put a needle in your vein and you may feel a slight pricking sensation," the door to the patient's room opens, and the chief resident enters with a group of junior residents and medical students.

The chief resident says, "Why are you bothering talking to that patient? Can't you see he is comatose?" Stacy replies that she realizes the patient is comatose and understands that in this condition, the sense of hearing is often the last sense to go. The chief resident laughs and says, "Well, he has been comatose for almost six months, so you better talk a lot louder." This comment elicits laughter from the junior residents and medical students as well.

Stacy turns back to the patient and restates her intention to insert the needle. She then draws the blood and leaves the room.

Your Role: Put yourself in Stacy's shoes. You decide to meet with the chief resident later in the day at a time appropriate for both of you. How could you use the CCGA model to discuss his behavior in front of the junior residents and medical students and lack of respect for both you and the patient?

BIBLIOGRAPHY

Beyerlein, Michael, Craig McGee, Gerald Klein, Jill Nemiro, and Laurie Broedling, eds. *The Collaborative Work Systems Field Book*. San Francisco: Jossey-Bass, 2003.

Carlson, Richard. *Don't Sweat the Small Stuff, and It's All Small Stuff*. New York: Hyperion, 1997.

Covey, Stephen R. *The Seven Habits of Highly Effective People*. New York: Simon and Schuster, 1989.

Crum, Thomas. *The Magic of Conflict: Turning a Life of Work into a Work of Art*. New York: Touchstone, 1987.

Domenici, Kathy. *Mediation: Empowerment in Conflict Management*. Prospect Heights: Waveland Press, Inc, 1996.

Ivancevich, John M., and Michael T. Matteson. *Organizational Behavior and Management (6th Ed.)*. New York: McGraw Hill, 2002.

Kouzes, James M., and Barry Z. Posner. *Credibility: How Leaders Gain and Lose It, Why People Demand It*. San Francisco: Jossey-Bass, 2003.

Levine, Stewart R. *Getting to Resolution: Turning Conflict into Collaboration*. San Francisco: Berrett-Koehler, 1998.

Loehr, Jim, and Tony Schwartz. *The Power of Full Engagement*. New York: Free Press, 2003.

Pickering, Peg. *How to Manage Conflict: Turn All Conflicts into Win-Win Outcomes*. Franklin Lakes: Career Press, 1999.

Slaikeu, Karl, and Ralph Hasson. *Controlling the Costs of Conflict*. San Francisco: Jossey-Bass, 1998.

Townsend, Terri. "Break the bullying cycle." *American Nurse Today* Vol. 7 No. 1 (January 2012), https://www.americannursetoday.com/break-the-bullying-cycle/.

ABOUT THE AUTHORS

Dr. Garry McDaniel is professor and program chair for the graduate and undergraduate degrees in human resource management at Franklin University, teaches in the international MBA program, and is a frequent speaker and trainer at conferences and corporate events worldwide. Dr. McDaniel has led numerous large-scale training efforts and global leadership and succession planning for a semiconductor manufacturer, and has authored six books.

- *Conflict Management in the Healthcare Profession*
- *High Performance Team Activities for Coaches*
- *The Dog's Guide to Your Happiness*
- *High Performance Coaching Techniques*
- *Conflict to Cooperation: A Process for Mediating Group Differences*
- *Managing the Business: How Successful Managers Align Management Systems with Business Strategy*

Dr. Gary Stroud is an innovative thinker and influential leader who takes a methodical approach to problems and organizational vision, and has the ability to inspire followers. He is committed to continuous improvement in organizational effectiveness and human-capital development, customer service, and the development of future leaders. Gary is a successful business leader with expertise in human-capital development and talent management; compensation and benefits; leadership, team, and organizational development; employee and customer experience; building high-performance cultures; custom assessments, executive coaching, and succession planning; employee engagement; employee health and wellness; and leading complex change initiatives. Gary is also an executive leadership advisor, coach, and consultant to CEOs, CHROs, COOs, CFOs, CTOs, executive teams, business owners, and boards of directors. He has a record of significantly improving employee engagement, morale, satisfaction, productivity, and retention while creating a unique high-performance culture.

Dr. Leslie Mathew has over thirty-three years' experience as a leader and academic in the healthcare industry, having worked across the globe. After completing his MD in 1979, he earned a master's in biotechnology enterprise from Johns Hopkins University and had the privilege of completing the executive MBA program from the Fisher College of Business while working as administrative director of operations at the Ohio State University Medical Center.

As a professor for the DHA program and chair of the MHA and MBA healthcare programs at Franklin University, Leslie encourages his graduate and doctoral students to achieve higher levels of excellence. He has been an active member of the university's Faculty Development Committee for the past eight years, and has led the group as committee chair for two years. He serves on different national and professional committees with organizations like the American College of Healthcare Executives (ACHE) and the Association of University Programs in Health Administration (AUPHA). He chaired the Local Program Council for ACHE at Columbus for two years, and continues to be an active member in planning their educational programs. Dr. Mathew earned the FACHE credential to become a Fellow of the College, and has served for two years on the editorial board of the *Journal of Healthcare Management*, a prestigious peer-reviewed journal of ACHE. He is also a member of the ACHE Regents Advisory Council, and has won two Service Recognition Awards from ACHE.

Dr. Mathew is an entertaining speaker, an effective trainer, and has a thriving practice to help leaders enhance their soft skills. He is an advocate for lifelong learning, has won multiple awards for teaching excellence, and takes delight in training adult working students and professionals from around the world.

Dr. Mikhail Dernakovski is a licensed doctor of psychiatry, psychotherapist, and former surgeon. Dr. Dernakovski is also the co-founder and master coach for the International Coach Union (ICU) and founder of coaching institutes in Moscow, St. Petersburg, Vilnius, Riga, Warsaw, Minsk, and Kiev. He a professional coach for executives in top international companies and has conducted more than 1,000 coaching and training events. His professional background includes psychiatry, psychotherapy (including cognitive-behavioral therapy, catalytic-imaginative and gestalt psychotherapy) and he has a second doctoral degree in psychology with specialized applications to management and business.

Dr. Alex Batsenko is a practicing urologist in Minsk, Belarus. Dr. Batsenko completed his MD at Belarusian State Medical University in 1994 and his practical training at Barsilai Medical Center in Israel in 2000. In 2012 he co-founded a medical center, SANTE, one of the first private medical centers in Belarus, and has earned the highest qualification category in urology and healthcare management. Dr. Batsenko has over twenty-five years' experience as an operating urologist and is considered one of the top physicians in the country. He is frequently invited to medical shows and health programs at National Belarus TV as a medical expert where he conducts seminars on urology and healthcare. Dr. Batsenko is a member of the European Association of Urologists and a strong advocate for enhancing the culture of medical practice and services to ensure the best-quality experience for patients and to create excellent working conditions for all healthcare practitioners.

Dr. Siddarth Agrawal is a medical doctor, and a graduate of the Faculty of Medicine at Wroclaw Medical University and the School of Chinese Medicine in Qingdao, China. He is a practicing physician at University Hospital in Wroclaw and an academic teacher at the Medical University in Wroclaw. He was awarded the

Supertalent in Medicine 2019 award by *Puls Medycyny* magazine for his outstanding clinical and scientific work. He is a grant holder of the National Science Center (NCN), the Ministry of Science and Higher Education (MNiSW), and the National Center for Research and Development (NCBiR), and the author and co-author of several patents awarded gold medals during the International Inventors' Fair Nuremberg and Warsaw. He is also laureate of the honorary distinction of the Polish Academy of Sciences Medical Laurel Wacław Mayzyl, and scholarship holder of the minister of health and minister of science and higher education.

CPSIA information can be obtained
at www.ICGtesting.com
Printed in the USA
LVHW040010230723
753139LV00004B/75